VALUE EDUCATION FOR AN AGE OF CRISIS

Betty A. Sichel
C. W. Post Center
Long Island University

UNIVERSITY
PRESS OF
AMERICA

PREFACE

This monograph by Betty A. Sichel is an
important part of a program by the Ellis
L. Phillips Foundation to clarify the
values of contemporary American society.

We started out in 1975 with agreement in
our board that American values are fragmented and uncertain. "Perhaps in the
bicentennial year we could return to the
wording of the Declaration of Independence,
'We hold these truths to be self-evident...'
and assist in a re-exploration of what
these truths are today."

We had in mind the national motto, "E
Pluribus UNUM" and we thought that if we
better understood the different values
now current in American society we could
inform and stimulate to restore that
covenant on which society ultimately depends.

We thought of education, religion and
economics as the best "disciplines in
which to test these values...a yeasty
mix."

After much discussion within our board
and with thinkers at Teachers' College
Columbia University, the National Council
of Churches and some of our great service
organizations we concluded that we should
focus our inquiry on three areas:

> Values in business decision making.
> Values in the arts and religion.
> Values in education.

All three have important moral implications.

The Foundation supported interdisciplinary
seminars and an Award Program at our neighbor C. W. Post Center of Long Island
University to bring together faculty and
businessmen to clarify what business can
and should do to improve our society "beyond the bottom line."

In the arts and religion we worked with
Christ Church United Methodist, New York
City. The key elements in this project
were lecture-demonstrations of how religious
values have been clarified, preserved and
transmitted over many centuries in various
art forms.

In education the Foundation commissioned
this monograph to bring the lay reader up
to date on how values are studied and conveyed in a pluralistic society.

Ellis L. Phillips Jr.
Jericho, Long Island, New York
January 1982

Copyright © 1982 by

University Press of America, Inc.

P.O. Box 19101, Washington, D.C. 20036

Library of Congress Catalog Card Number: 81-40642

CONTENTS

74541

INTRODUCTION

Recent books, essays, and speeches by academic and political leaders echo one theme: American society is in trouble.[1] We have been told that a malaise has swept over the country, that people no longer are committed to the basic American values, and that the values which made this country powerful and important no longer exist. Further, we are told that the American family--the bastion of American values--no longer provides the warmth, comfort, care, and sustenance necessary for value education and personal growth. With numerous liberals deserting liberal causes, neo-conservatives and conservatives have formed a "new class" to retreat and espouse "the good old" values. In this book, I do not want to repeat the criticism leveled against American life or heap accolades on the values of bygone days. Rather than offering yet another critique, I shall search for the meaning of the present value crisis and delineate methods by which the average individual can initiate value education in his family, school and community.

Earliest recorded thought reveals concern with morality and how human beings should conduct their lives. The Old and New Testaments are often interpreted as presenting a codified set of rules which should govern each human life. Whether humanity is confronted with tragedy, joy, anger or compassion, hate or love, the Bible provides a moral vision for all people.

In classical Greece, humans peered inward. Poets and philosophers, politicians and historians, the famous and unknown all wondered about virtue, justice, courage and wisdom. They wondered why an individual's deeds so often fell short of his words. They wondered about the boundaries between public and private life and about the limits of individual rights. At a time of war and cruelty, they preached the doctine of the mean, "nothing in excess." There was an odd contrast: On one side a slave's testimony in court was valid only if he had been tortured. On the other hand, the free citizen sought justice and virtue in deed, word, and character. In war, weak cities were expected to follow the dictates of the strongest states. At the same time, politicians in these strong states continued to extol the merits of democracy.

1

In the Republic, Plato speaks of these embarrassing and incomprehensible aspects of human life, discovering that the just person often appears unjust while the unjust person appears just. The unjust person even seems to profit and possess the happier life when compared with the just person. It was said that:

> . . . the just man who has such a disposition will be whipped; he'll be racked; he'll be bound; he'll have both eyes burned out; and, at the end, when he has undergone every sort of evil, he'll be crucified.[2]

On the other hand, the truly unjust ". . . does not wish to seem unjust, but to be unjust . . ."[3] Thus, there is no crime or behavior from which the unjust shrinks. His rewards, however, seem great:

> First, he rules in the city because he seems to be just. Then he takes in marriage from whatever station he wants and gives in marriage to whomever he wants; he contracts and has partnerships with whomever he wants, and, besides benefiting himself in all this, he gains because he has no qualms about doing injustice.[4]

The unjust person plays a subtle and wily game, appearing just to many and gaining the good fortunes of life, honor, power, wealth, and happiness. The youth of Plato's society asked him, "Why should we be just?" "Why is justice preferable to injustice?" Today, our youths ask the same questions and wonder whether our society's morality has progressed beyond that of Plato's society.

Throughout human history, these same contradictions and questions constantly reappear. Theoretical moral ideals are high; rarely, however, does moral conduct become even a pale shadow of the ideal. Little similarity exists between words and deeds and between idealized moral standards and reality. Many words have been written about the right, just, good, evil, sinful, temperate, courageous, and wicked. In the numerous codes, discussions, doctrines, and arguments about morality, one word was used infrequently until the latter third of the nineteenth century. That word is "value." At the present time, individual values, value education, and the state of societal values are frequently discussed. How the term "value" became such a popular concept is one of the interesting stories in the history of ideas. The story suggests why the boundary of societal and educational concern shifted from the moral domain to the much wider value domain.

Until the latter third of the nineteenth century, the concept "value" was associated only with the field of economics. In England, Adam Smith did not use the term "value" to clarify any aspect of his moral theory, but allowed his economic theory to monopolize the concept. In Germany, as well, "value" was an economic concept. A revised use of the term "value" actually signalled a reaction against predominant ethical theory, a revolution against centuries of established thought. Standards, ideals, and principles rested on an objective foundation based on the word of God, religious doctrine and texts, and Platonic unchanging, eternal ideals. In the eighteenth century, Kant launched a Copernican revolution in ethics, but though he recognized the primacy of human beings, his two categorical imperatives still retained the objective bias of earlier religious and absolutist ethics. One categorical imperative states that each human being should be treated as an end in himself, never as a means and the other imperative mandates that all moral judgments should be made universal. That is, the individual making a moral judgment should accept the validity of the judgment for all similar cases. Since these two categorical imperatives were to stand behind any moral decision an individual made, a moral judgment could not be merely subjective or emotional. The rational and objective still reigned. More important, Kant's concern was with morality rather than values in general.

When psychology sprang from fertile German soil, it needed a quantitative, scientific way of judging situations and experiences relative to the individual human subject. Psychologists searched for concepts which not only revealed human desires, hopes, needs, intentions, and concerns but could be treated quantitatively. As a science, psychology wanted to escape the taint of the qualitative and externally objective, discoverable world. It wanted to focus on human beings and discern the laws and principles which undergird human life, yet are quantitatively valid. The concept "value" proved a most suitable candidate. Value had become a quantitative measure for economics; therefore, psychologists possessed the necessary quantitative component. Also, value, in economics, had referred to an infinite variety of objects or situations, thus, psychologists also possessed a concept which could be applied to any human concern.

In England, the Utilitarians concentrated on moral, political, and economic theories. For example, at the end of the nineteenth century, John Stuart Mill, in his famous On Liberty, restricts the power and jurisdiction of governments. According to Mill, an individual's private life, beliefs, and life style are his own. Only if his freedom and life style interfere with others should the individual be constrained. Not only did he criticize governmental interference in an individual's life, but Mill was equally critical of the restraint on the individual by the masses. Actually, tyranny by the masses might be even more dangerous than governmental restrictions. Insidiously and most often without thought, the masses could control the life style, forms of behavior, and beliefs of individuals. Even though Mill stressed the individual's right to his own private life without interference from government or others, he did not use the term "value" to speak of individual desires and needs. He did not self-consciously develop a theory of value. This concept was foreign to his moral writings.

However, in his political economy, Mill remains faithful to previously accepted economic stress on the concept "value," while attempting to dispel some of its ambiguity. Mill defines "the value or the exchange of a thing" as "its general power of purchasing; the command which its possession gives over purchasable commodities in general."[5] By concentrating on purchasing power, that is, value in use, as other economists before him, Mill accepted the necessity of a quantifiable conceptualization of value in economics.

The Utilitarians--Jeremy Bentham, James and John Mill--catalyzed social and political reform and motivated the passage of laws to improve the life of the average person. In this way, they promoted the dream of the greatest happiness for the many. Happiness was not merely the right of the few, the aristocracy, elite or powerful. Happiness was the right of all human beings. For Bentham, a calculus of happiness would guarantee scientific exactitude and democratic equal treatment. Even without the right to control private life, government could still influence conditions leading to greater private happiness for the masses through betterment of health care and the improvement of education.

In spite of the quantitative predilections of Utilitarians and the surge for social and political reform, value theory never found a particularly hospitable climate in England. English philosophers preferred to work within traditional moral categories of right, good, duty and responsibility. Thus value theory emigrated to the United States. As with so many other European discoveries and revolutions, value theory came into its own, and gained new meaning and strength in the American intellectual climate.

American psychologists and philosphers quickly recognized that there were three distinct ways of looking at values. First, values could be viewed as objective characteristics, inherent in objects and external to human beings. Second, values could be internal to human beings, or subjective. Third, values could be a matter of interaction or transaction between a human being and some thing, situation, or state of affairs. No matter which view is accepted, it is difficult to decide why or how human beings value something. Is it merely an emotional response or intuition? Is there some objective method and standard of evaluation, or do conditioning, past experience or external pressure determine an individual's values?

During the first half of the twentieth century, philosophers attempted to clarify these and other theoretical problems relating to values and value theory.

Some writers attempted to discern which values Americans held in common. Even as late as 1949, the historian, Henry Steele Commager, spoke of the characteristics common to all Americans:

The American is optimistic, self-confident,
and self-satisfied. He takes for granted
that his is the best of all countries, the
happiest and most virtuous of societies,
the richest and most bounteous of all
economies . . . . Although less sure of

5

progress than his fathers or grandfathers,
he is confident that if there is progress,
it will be under American leadership and
bear the American imprint. Accustomed to
seeing his boldest plans and most sanguine
anticipations realized he believes that
they will continue to be fulfilled.[6]

In 1958, the sociologist, Robert Cooley Angell,
posited the following set of American values:

> Dignity of the person including equality
> before the law
> Civil and religious liberties
> Responsible democracy--control by the
> people of their common life
> Opportunity for all
> Humanitarianism and friendliness
> A high level of effort
> Competition within fair rules
> Technological progress
> Peaceful orientation toward other nations
> Patriotism[7]

This commonality of values was fundamental to the "melting pot" thesis which assumed that various ethnic and
religious groups, different socio-economic levels and
waves of immigrants, urban and agrarian populations
could be molded into a single, harmonious, democratic
society with one set of values. In recent years, the
futility of this belief in a homogeneous society and
set of values has been argued. The trend has been to
claim the vitality, viability, and strength of pluralistic value systems. Equally strong, however, is the
argument that fundamental values are not easily destroyed. Even when individuals seem to convert to new values,
the old ones constantly reappear.[8] The present rever-
beration, confusion, and growth tremors felt by society
could be caused by new and different pluralistic interpretations of the core values.

The trend toward value pluralism has not quelled
voices of criticism. Today, a common chorus chants
about the erosion of values in American society. Many
individuals are blamed for the degeneration of societal
and personal values: Politicians are blamed for undermining popular belief in democratic procedures through
graft, chicanery, and lies; business managers and

leaders are blamed for adding to environmental pollution; the average citizen is blamed for wasting energy
and other key resources. Can the value crisis be
blamed on any single group? The value crisis is further underscored by the quantity and variety of societal
problems; professional misconduct; continuing social,
political, and economic inequities; the frailty of American institutions, whether family or school; the level
of violence, child abuse, drug and alcohol addiction,
and suicide; disenchantment with the American work
ethos; the abandonment of the vision of the good life
for the poor; the increase in white collar crime.

How should children be educated so that they are
prepared to deal with various value problems? Can education suggest ways to resolve the present value crisis?
Which institution should be charged with value educa-
tion--home, school, or greater society? Can the family
contend with value problems and implement meaningful
value education? In recent years, the nuclear American
family itself has been so beleaguered that family life
in its traditional extended or nuclear form may no longer possess the inherent value or solidarity it once
possessed. If there has been a breakdown of the traditional family, must other groups foster value education? What is the role of the school in such education?
Since formal schooling does not operate in a vacuum,
other societal institutions--even business and professional groups--affect the success of value education in
school.

Over 2000 years ago, classical Greeks wondered
whether virtue could be taught. If so, who were the
teachers of value in society? In one of Plato's
dialogues, Protagoras explains how virtue is taught.
Society and citizens:

> . . . teach and admonish . . . (individuals)
> from earliest childhood til the last day of
> their lives. As soon as one of them grasps
> what is said to him, the nurse, the mother,
> the tutor, and the father himself strive
> hard that the child may excel, and as each
> act and word occurs they teach and impress
> upon him that this is just, and that unjust,
> one thing noble, another base . . . and that
> he is to do this and not do that . . . After

this they send him to school and charge
the master to take far more pains over
their children's good behaviour than
over their letters . . .[9]

And when they are released from
schooling the city compels them to
learn the laws and to live according
to them. . . , that their conduct may
not be swayed by their own light fancies...[10]

(E)veryone is a teacher of virtue. . . .[11]

Important here is the view that value or moral education is not the sole province of one segment of society.
An individual's value or moral education does not result from the limited concern of one institution, the
school. Rather, all of society's institutions and all
segments of social life-parents and teachers, friends
and employers, laws and customs, television and news-
papers--contribute to the values accepted by an individual. Although schools and teachers have a fundamental
responsibility for value education, parents and concerned citizens cannot assume their own efforts are
unimportant or irrelevant. They play critical roles
in determining the values, the attitudes, behavior,
standards, desires, beliefs and interest of children
and youth. Adults influence and determine the character and quality of value education, even if they consciously shun this role.

As an undertaking of the utmost importance,
value education is fraught with difficulties. Merely
an announcement of the inclusion of a value education
course in a school causes many communities to become
emotionally involved and hostile to the undertaking,
without even knowing the course content. What is actually taught when a school presents a course called
"value education?" Dividing the expression "value
education" into its two component words does not sim-
plify the question. The term "value" is ambiguous and
susceptible to a variety of uses and meanings. The word
"chair", a concrete object, refers to a considerable
number of inanimate objects of different size, design,
and color. Yet, in most instances, it is fairly easy
to discern which object is a chair. Though the word
"dog" refers to both the animate and inanimate, we have
little difficulty identifying dogs, whether large or
small, porcelain or in a photograph, our own or someone

8

else's pet. If a word does not signify concrete objects but qualities, its definitions become much more elusive. When words such as "quick" or "slow" are used in conversation, misunderstandings often occur. Even here, however, some agreement is possible. If someone claims a runner ran a "fast" or "slow" race, clarification easily specifies the meaning of these terms. For example, the runner may be fast or slow in comparison with his own previous record or in relation to school or international records. It is more difficult to define words like "kind," "liar," "just," "inconsiderate," and "wrong." From earliest writings, volumes have attempted to clarify the use and meaning of justice, good, right and wrong. Not only philosophy but religious writings and literature have been concerned with such value terms. For example, in Euripides' tragedy, Hippolytus, Phaedra puzzles about the things of value in life when she says:

> Many a time in night's long empty spaces
> I have pondered on the causes of a life's
> shipwreck,
> I think that our lives are worse than the
> mind's quality would warrant. There are
> many who know virtue.
> We know the good, we apprehend it clearly.
> But we can't bring it to achievement. Some
> are betrayed by their own laziness, and
> others value some other pleasures above
> virtue.
> There are many pleasures in a woman's life--
> long gossiping talks and leisure.[12]

Here Phaedra was wondering whether rational choice or emotions determined values and which values were most important in a woman's life. Today, this same questioning occurs. We do not agree about what should be valued. And we do not agree about the meaning of various value terms, whether good or bad, right or wrong, beautiful or ugly.

It is no easier to discern the boundaries of value education. Which of the following are examples of the content of value education--the value of jewelry; the value of family, friends, and companions; the value of higher education and concern with self-improvement; the value of a pollution-free environment or of energy use, no matter the cost to life and health?

Though schools are expected to teach a child basic skills of reading, writing, and arithmetic, the school's responsibility in relation to value education is not at all obvious. Can formal education by itself change, modify, or negate values formed during informal education? A more baffling and sensitive issue is whether schools have a right to change, clarify, or modify an individual's values. Some have argued that value education is not limited to a single subject entitled "value education," but infiltrates all formal education.

In a well known court case, Wisconsin v. Yoder et al, the Amish argued against compulsory school attendance laws. The Amish contended that formal education per se, scientific knowledge and vocational skills, exposed children to values antagonistic to those of the Amish community and thus contributed to undermining their society.

> With set limits to the amount of knowledge
> a young person can acquire on one hand, and
> with the dread of censure . . . on the other,
> one can scarcely find a more effective way of
> bounding the little (Amish) community . . .
> Limited knowledge preserves the existing
> order of things; it reinforces traditional
> values by keeping alternate courses of
> action to a minimum. Traditional values
> and stereotypes are thus maintained by un-
> familiarity with alternate courses of action.
> Furthermore, questions about in-group prac-
> tices are kept to a minimum.[13]

The Supreme Court not only upheld the right of the Amish to withdraw their children from school after the eighth grade, but tacitly recognized how formal education itself influenced the values of children. Part of the summary by Justice Berger for six members of the Court states:

> Secondary schooling, by exposing, goals,
> and values contrary to sincere religious
> beliefs, and by substantially interfering
> with the religious beliefs development of
> the Amish child and his integration into
> the way of life of the Amish faith commun-
> ity at the crucial adolescent state of

development, contravened the basic religious
tenets and practice of the Amish faith, both
as to the parent and the child; . . .[14]

The Amish values, upheld by the Court, were based on
Amish religious beliefs, which wholly determined their
life style.

While the values and beliefs of groups must be
protected and the school does not have the right to
indoctrinate, schools cannot assume value neutrality.[15]
A hidden curriculum of values surrounds students. It
includes such elements as the way a teacher dresses,
whether a teacher smiles or frowns, the books in a
classroom, the decorations or lack of decorations on
walls, the examples presented during a lesson, the implementation of rules in classes and school, the after-
school activities, and the attention or lack of attention to holidays. Since schools cannot avoid a value
orientation, their only option is to know which values
are implicity transmitted, and to judge whether these
are the values the school should advocate. If schools
desire to influence and educate students, the schools
themselves must constantly be self-conscious about
their value choices.

This same self-consciousness concerning values is
necessary for any community organization. An example
of such awareness is the recent image change by the
Girl Scouts of America. Instead of remaining an organization catering to middle-class, white Americans, the
Girl Scouts are now a multiracial, multi-ethnic organization. In order to maintain their basic commitments,
the development of values, self-awareness, altruism,
and social awareness, the Girl Scouts have examined
their own values and their own social consciousness.
This examination led to changes in membership, different ways of conducting meetings and an expansion of
leadership and programs.[16]

This book seeks to assist any individual, group,
school, organization, teacher, parent, or leader interested in such value awareness and value education.
Prior to investigating the methods of value education,
a number of preliminary problems are studied: (i) What
are the roots of the value crisis? (ii) What are the
boundaries of values? (iii) What framework can be
useful for understanding the diverse methods of value

11

education?

The major concern of this first section is to respond to the questions: Can the pluralistic values of different groups and individuals be blended together into a unified, interlocking whole? Is it possible for a society to retain and accept pluralistic values together with a unified set of basic values? These questions are asked to reinforce the assumption of this presentation: <u>A</u> <u>society</u> <u>or</u> <u>nation</u> <u>cannot</u> <u>survive</u> <u>and</u> <u>progress</u> <u>without</u> <u>some</u> <u>common</u> <u>basic</u> <u>values</u> <u>and</u> <u>common</u> <u>moral</u> <u>principles</u>.

The second section of the book is devoted to value development and methods of value education. No single theory is proposed as the best method. Rather, the reader is presented with some leading theories of value development and education. It will be argued that no single theory in itself provides the basis for value education.

NOTES

1. For example, Christopher Lasch, The Culture of Narcissism; American Life in an Age of Diminishing Expectations (New York: W. W. Norton & Co., Inc., 1978); David Ehrenfeld, The Arrogance of Humanism (New York: Oxford University Press, 1978).

2. Rep. II, 361E-362A (Bloom trans.).

3. Ibid. 362A

4. Ibid. 362B (my italics).

5. John Stuart Mill, Principles of Political Economy, 5th ed. (New York: D. Appleton and Co., 1880), p. 538.

6. Henry Steele Commager, "Portrait of the American," Years of the Modern: An American Appraisal, John W. Chase, ed. (New York: Longmans, Green & Co., 1949), p. 8.

7. Robert Cooley Angell, Free Society and Moral Crisis (Ann Arbor: Ann Arbor Paperbacks, 1965 [1958]), p. 22.

8. Ibid., p. 57.

9. Protagoras 325C-E (Lamb trans.).

10. Ibid., 326D

11. Ibid., 327E (my italics).

12. "Hippolytus," 276ff (Lattimore trans.).

13. John A. Hostetler, Amish Society (Baltimore: Johns Hopkins Press, 1963), pp. 144-145.

14. Wisconsin v. Jonas Yoder et al. (380US, at 192-193, 13L Ed 2d at 751, 752). This case is discussed in Albert N. Keim, Compulsory Education and the Amish (Boston: Beacon Press, 1975).

15. Norma V. Overly, ed., The Unstudied Curriculum: Its Impact on Children (Washington, D. C.: Association for Supervision and Curriculum Development, 1970).

16. Maureen Early, "Look What They're Doing Now," <u>News-
day</u>, Part II (February 13, 1978), pp. 4-6.

CHAPTER I

THE ROOTS OF OUR VALUE CRISIS

Though current concern about the state of values seems unique, similar concerns and questions have been repeated periodically. In the aftermath of great social or political struggles and upheavals, following great discoveries or cataclysmic changes, human beings seek regeneration for their lives. Are old values valid for new conditions and developments? With ethnic diversity and historic change, are there still values which remain an intrinsic part of the great values chain linking all of human life? Simultaneously with societal value changes, each individual's life also undergoes change, requiring modification of that individual's values. Sickness, unemployment, marriage, the birth of children, new employment responsibilities, education--all cause an individual to review his values and to relate different-ly to other people's values.

Recent books studying mid-life and old-age crises and personal development point to changing values throughout individual lives. For example, Gail Sheehy's book, Passages, is appropriately sub-titled "Predictable Crises of Adult Life." Each episode examines not merely a career or marital change, but as often a radical up-heaval of values. John DeLorean, the wonderboy of General Motors, was once at an ordinary automotive show when he suddenly thought:

> "Here I was spending my life bending the fenders a little differently to try to con-vince the public they were getting a new and dramatically different product. What gross excesses! It was ridiculous. . . There's got to be more to life than this."[1]

Though many outsiders would have judged him a success, DeLorean questioned the values guiding his life. At the height of his career, corporate vice-president, DeLorean resigned to follow a more satisfying life style and set of values. This story of changing life values is not the exception, but a common example of the radical changes confronting many adults at the present time.

15

Just as value crisis and change is common in the life of the individual or society, the tendency toward value unification and the restoration of value harmony is equally strong. Neither a society nor an individual can tolerate ongoing, unceasing value chaos and challenge. The present societal value crisis may momentarily blind us to the commonalities within value pluralism. The confusion of seemingly inconsistent values may hinder us from recognizing any potentiality for value unity; however, the roots of such value unity exist within the present situation. Our first endeavor is to look at the changes in values and discover overall causes for the current concern with values and value education. Then, from these diverse elements and pluralistic values, a unified value vision can be sought.

The state of values in American society can be evaluated in different ways. For example, history may be viewed as little more than the ongoing struggle to retain, change, or modify values. Only with difficulty have human beings retained civilizing and humanizing values. At every juncture, there have been possibilities for values degeneration and a return to primitive or barbaric life. Some may claim that values have never before reached such a high pinnacle. Never before have so many had such a high level of cultural enjoyment, material comfort, education, medical care and political enfranchisement. Still others speak of the demise of common values and the loss of individual control over almost every aspect of life. At present, this last interpretation seems to represent the majority opinion. This view also implies that there is a value crisis. Considerable verbiage has already attempted to explain how our values have disintegrated. The normal vicissitudes of time have not merely eroded out-of-date values, but at an accelerating rate values have deteriorated and disintegrated.

Concrete examples of the value crisis seem easily discernible. Political scheming, increased violence and crime, the break-up of the nuclear family, and accelerating divorce rates are just a few. Instead of looking at the concrete symptoms of our present value crisis, this chapter proposes to search for the deeper, underlying causes of the crisis. Three different perspectives--the historical, sociological and ontological-- provide focuses through which the complexity of the value crisis is revealed. One additional idea first must be clarified, this being the meaning of the

expression "value crisis." If the present period is
experiencing a value crisis, what are the dimensions
of a crisis? Even though many argue there is a value
crisis, is this actually the case? Are we confronting
a value crisis?

What is a crisis?

Webster's Unabridged Dictionary's first definition
of crisis is "the turning point for better or worse in
an acute disease or fever." In its other general definitions, Webster's refers to a crisis as being a "decisive moment," a "turning point," which will determine
the future consequences or status of a situation. In
an individual's life, there may be a series of crises,
whether physical, psychological, or developmental.
During previous centuries, the idea of an adolescent
crisis of sturm und drang became popular. Numerous
adolescents identified with Goethe's Young Man Werther
and followed Werther's model; rejected in love and
searching for identity, they too committed suicide.
This type of crisis experience became the benchmark of
the adolescent crisis in general. However, the adolescent crisis is better expressed through the crisis
experienced by Meaulnes in Fournier's The Wanderer.
Meaulnes, an adolescent, rebels against life and runs
away from school. He discovers his dream life, a palace
where a perpetual party is attended only by beautiful,
elegantly clothed children and kindly grandparents.
What is more fitting for the adolescent who wants to
mature and yet retain the purity of childhood and the
kindliness of grandparents! Suddenly, Meaulnes is
separated from the palace. Though he searches, he never
again discovers it as it was. When finally he does happen upon the palace, it has changed. At last, he must
mature and accept adult responsibilities.[2] Similarly,
the adolescent at first wavers between childhood and
adulthood. Only with the resolution of this developmental crisis does the adolescent achieve his identity.

At present, psychologists claim adolescents are
not the only ones facing developmental crises. Led by
Erik Erikson, psychologists now study the life crises
occurring at different critical junctures during adulthood. Gail Sheehy speaks of this:

"What do I want out of this life, now that
I'm doing what I ought to do."
A restless vitality wells up as we approach

17

30. Almost everyone wants to make some
alteration. If he has been dutifully per-
forming in his corporate slit, he may
suddenly feel too narrowed and restricted.
If he has been in a long period of training, such as medicine, he may wonder at
this point if life is all work and no play.
If she has been at home with children, she
itches to expand her horizons. . . . The
impulse to broaden often leads us to action
even before we know what we are missing.[3]

However, our concern here is not predominantly
with the value crises of specific individuals, but the
general value crisis confronting American society.
Webster's Unabridged Dictionary posits another definition of crisis, which is closer to our needs:

a psychological or social condition characterized by unusual instability caused
by excessive stress and either endangering
or felt to endanger the continuity of the
individual or his group: esp: such a social
condition requiring the transformation of
existing cultural patterns and values.

A social or political crisis does not necessarily suggest the demise of society. In the United States,
there has always been fear that democratic life could
be extinguished by either reactionary or radical
factions. Even though Alexis de Tocqueville in the
nineteenth century noted many features advantageous
to the continuance of American democracy, he also recognized its fragility.[4]

The Historical Perspective.

Though the Vietnam War seemed to create value
problems of major proportion, the Second World War was
the real watershed of the current value crisis. Instead of the normal trickle of societal value problems,
war catalyzes diverse elements which might have remained dormant for many years. For example, prior to the
Second World War, certain theoretical scientific advancements made possible the construction of the atomic
bomb. Only the exigencies of war motivated the financial support and technological effort necessary for its
development. With the development of military weaponry

came the promise of cheap, safe energy for the masses. Yet, at the end of the war, technological and scientific advancement not only contributed to the betterment of human life, but increased the problems faced by society. In the case of nuclear energy, for example, at present there are numerous positions and debates regarding its safety, feasibility, and desirability.

In the course of many generations, value problems are usually confined to certain limited dimensions. During "normal" periods, human beings evolve with changing environments and resolve what may be termed "manageable problems." Individuals may even confront and successfully resolve crises of incredible proportions. However, in most cases, the crisis is of a limited time span and has limited physical dimensions, e.g., a natural catastrophe. External assistance lightens individual burdens and provides a directing leadership. Furthermore, the individual perceives the exact problem. Even if solutions are not readily available, the features of the problem are apparent. The starving seek food, the homeless shelter. But with war the dimensions change. Instead of a limited number of problems within a limited time span, value problems proliferate within an extremely short time. Segments of the population are given roles they never possessed and are unwilling to yield after the war. Sudden changes in population affect every social, political, and economic aspect of society. This has been the way of wars in general; the pace of change during each war creates conditions with which society and individuals cannot cope. In fact, with the increased quantity of potential problems, individuals rarely perceive the causes of confusion or chaos in their own or societal life.

These consequences of war have caused value crises whether we look back over 2000 years or confine ourselves to American history. For example, over 2000 years ago, the Persian War required capitalization and resources not available to Athens from the landed aristocracy. From silver mining at Laurium, Athens not only generated capital to construct a fleet, but catalyzed individual financial speculation.[5] With newly acquired wealth, Athens became the financial and trade center of Greece. Individuals possessed the means to purchase goods--household goods, armour, and better education. Though democracy already existed in Athens, newly acquired wealth caused individuals to ask, why shouldn't money also purchase new rights and increased social and political power?

Similarly, the Second World War required previously unimagined outlays of capital. A nation still struggling to revive itself from the great depression in no way had the liquid capital and resources to finance a war. The capitalization problems were partially resolved through loans and credit. At war's end, newly married couples searched for ways to finance the purchase of homes. Mortgages with small cash outlays were made available. It took little imagination to move from bank financing of houses, cars and major appliances to the instant loans of credit cards for the purchase of the most miniscule item. This ability to finance the purchase of a dollar or ten thousand dollar item meant that new segments of society found it easier to purchase material goods and finance various business, education, and leisure activities. From this group emerged individuals demanding additional rights and political and social power.

Emphasis here does not suggest that economy alone explains all value crises. Just as easily, one could begin from another direction and still demonstrate the effect of war on a society's values. During a war, the values of other societies and cultures become exceptionally visible. Prior to the Second World War, the United States insulated itself and concentrated primarily on internal problems and affairs. The war negated such protectionism and isolationism. Suddenly, the variety and relativity of values were forced on large segments of the population. Protected, parochial youth became aware of many unknown distant ways of life and appreciated radically different values and life styles. They began questioning the sacredness of their own hallowed values.

With each American War, formal and informal education was extended to include a larger portion of the population. Better educated individuals questioned values previously taken for granted. Following the Second World War, the GI Bill of Rights opened the doors of universities and technical schools to large numbers of students. With changes in their educational and socio-economic levels, these individuals' values also changed.

For example, the average American soldier overseas during the Second World War missed and valued the following:

A fresh lettuce and tomato sandwich with ice cold fresh milk to wash it down. Fresh milk and the morning papers at the front door. The smell of a drugstore. A train and the engine whistle.[6]

Yet, when these soldiers returned home, they modified their values.[7] No longer would these youths merely love:

White plates and cups, clean-gleaming,
Ringed with blue lines; and feathery, faery dust;
Wet roofs, beneath the lamp-light; the strong crust
Of friendly bread; and many tasting foods.[8] . . .

What were the new values? Gourmet cooking and painting, owning a private home and a boat, involvement in civic affairs and service agencies, attending the theatre and vacationing overseas, playing golf and tennis, attending museums and concerts--all these and many more were the values of the new American. What does this shift from pre-war to post-war values suggest? Is this merely the destruction of the older Puritan work ethic, or is this the development of a new hedonistic, pleasure living, self-interested American value system?

History does not provide easy answers, and history alone does not allow us to understand which new value orientation is developing.

The Sociological Perspective.

The sociologist Tönnies argues that social crisis has developed out of the movement from gemeinschaft to gessellschaft. Gemeinschaft refers to an agrarian society where life depended on trusting, familial, interpersonal relationships. Agreements were based on a handshake; mores and customs remained secure for generation after generation; behavior was enforced by the small agrarian community. Individuals were concerned with each other's joys and sorrows. Neighbors were not merely casual companions, ever-changing outsiders, but were considered family.

21

With the rise of industrialization and migration to cities, gesellschaft became the dominant characteristic of societal life. Contractual agreement replaced the handshake and an individual's word. The contract assumed fundamental importance in social interactions no matter how slight the event, situation, problem, or purchase. Furthermore, contracts determined one's societal role; no individual was expected to fulfill any role not stipulated by contract. The outcome of such specialization has had its tragic moments, e.g., when individuals stand aside during violent crimes, claiming it is not their role to become involved. Lives thus lived often become excessively individualistic and lonely. In massive apartment complexes, neighbors are unknown; each individual lives in anonymity and remains segregated from others. Obviously, the shift from gemeinschaft to gesellschaft caused radical shifts in values. The uprooting of a large rural and agrarian population and its resettlement in cities and suburbs caused a value crisis. Values which were appropriate for rural and farm life were no longer appropriate for urban and suburban life.

In an agrarian society there would be satisfaction with a job completed by oneself, whether sewing, milking cows, making furniture, or canning. And yet individuals would recognize and appreciate the value of others. The elderly were the respected leaders of the family; friends and neighbors contributed to each other's survival whether this included raising a roof or helping when sickness incapacitated a family member. Entertainment was gained through simple things such as good talk in front of a fireplace, a square dance, or work for a local church. A trip to a distant town or city was a rare treat, an experience to be shared with family and friends alike. Individuals were directly involved with the democratic process in their small town and county. Even if the federal or state government were far removed and not susceptible to personal influence, the individual could still control local political decisions. The day to day decisions which directly influenced the quality of personal life were made in one's own community. Government was participatory locally, even though representational nationally.

In urban society, the individual no longer protected himself and his neighbors, but resorted to specially trained personnel, to police and firefighters. Even though people have turned to complicated and expensive hobbies for personal satisfaction, they still rely on specialists for the resolution of many problems, for medical care and household repair, for beauty needs and gardening, for dentistry and decorating. People gained in mobility. They traveled to work--by car, train, and even airplane and boat. The trip that had been a once in a lifetime adventure became a daily habit. As long as the job seemed interesting, allowed for status, advancement, and perhaps, self-fulfillment, was financially lucrative and secure, the distance traveled between home and work became unimportant. In earlier times, rarely could the small town inhabitant see a show of itinerant performers which traveled from town to town. Suddenly, every home had one or more television sets, hi-fi equipment, and radios. Entertainment was varied and instantaneous. Each individual in a family could enjoy his own entertainment, practice his own skills, play at a different sport, read different books, and have different hobbies.

Does the sociological perspective suggest the identical radical shift as was suggested by the historical perspective? Does the new value orientation stress the self-centered, hedonistic individual, or is it necessary to search for common values which still bind all human beings in a single community or society?

The Ontological Perspective.

Turning from the historical and sociological to the ontological perspective reveals a far more menacing spectre. The ontological refers to those qualities and characteristics which are fundamental in the universe; for our purposes, those most basic elements characterizing the world for human beings. During the nineteenth century, philosophers, novelists, and social critics warned of an impending human crisis. The roots of the crisis were found in science. During earlier centuries, science had had limited visions and had existed within clearly defined boundaries. Suddenly, science intruded into every aspect of human life and society. Nothing was sacred ground on which science was forbidden to tread.

At present, the full force of this scientific and technological advancement is felt by all segments of society. Obviously, scientific discoveries have benefited human life, controlling disease, improving consumer goods, creating leisure activities, increasing knowledge and disseminating more knowledge. In addition,

23

however, these discoveries and advancements have surprised us with unexpected, unplanned, and undesirable
side-effects. At times, we even wonder whether the
good truly outweighs the bad. Science and technology
have been blamed for every conceivable problem in society; the knowledge explosion, the population explosion, diminishing individual privacy, the break-up of
the American family, the dehumanization of human beings,
the weakening of religious and spiritual life, the pollution of the air, rivers, and land.

Simultaneously, others claim that any wholesale
criticism of science and technology is unfair and in-
valid. Instead science and technology are lauded as
the panacea to perfect human life. Nothing is beyond
science's ability. With time, effort, financial support, and belief in science's powers, all the problems
besetting human life can be overcome.

Even value problems, some believe, are resolvable,
if the methods of science are utilized. At the beginning of the twentieth century, one scientist explained
this unbridled optimism, a belief in science's ability
to perfect moral life:

> Science alone builds solidly; it has built
> astronomy and physics; today it builds biology;
> by the same procedures tomorrow it will build
> ethics. Its rules hold undivided sway, no one
> can murmur against them; and a man will no
> more think of rebelling against the moral law
> than he thinks of rebelling against the theorem
> of the three perpendiculars or the law of gravi-
> tation.[9]

Though fewer thinkers today would give such overwhelming support, others do not blush when supporting
science's ability to perfect moral behavior. For example, B. F. Skinner begins his controversial book
Beyond Freedom and Dignity with the following statement:

> In trying to solve the terrifying problems
> that face us in the world today, we naturally
> turn to the things we do best. We play from
> strength, and our strength is science and
> technology.[10]

More cautious thinkers claim that science and technology are neutral in themselves. Human beings, they claim, decide whether to use science and technology for good or evil. Whichever view of science is accepted--positive, negative, or neutral--traditional values or morality must be reeling from the character and acceleration of science and technology.

For example, if medical science can cure or arrest certain diseases and can ameliorate health problems, the value issues confronting the public, whether patient or physician, must increase. Which individuals in society should receive exotic surgery and expensive treatment? Should all segments of society, no matter their socio-economic level, age, or education, be granted such medical care? If such equal care is a priority, should resources be diverted from other societal institutions and interests? If so, which ones? With increasingly sophisticated medical technology, other value problems must arise. In fact, value problems may arise which had never even been imagined.

If the changing nature and quantity of value problems is viewed from a different scientific discipline or perspective, the confusion of changing values can still be perceived. For example, current concern with ecology and pollution raises many value issues. Should the production and consumption of material and consumer goods be controlled to control both pollution and resource depletion? Who should be responsible for policing hazardous pollution conditions and for instituting necessary industrial and technological modifications-- the consumer, federal and state governments, the manufacturer, or independent agencies? No matter which scientific or technological enterprise is considered, a host of new, unresolved value problems and questions would arise. However, we can still revert to one of the original questions. Have science and technology really created the present value crisis?

To discover the underlying causes of this value crisis, the ontological perspective requires a deeper search. Science and technology are not the culprits. The value crisis is fueled by the frustrations and absurdities of human life and the difficulties each individual finds in his search for life's meaning. In his book, Working, Studs Turkel interviews people in all walks of life. Many spoke about their search for meaning and the absence of meaning in their lives and work. The tale of the dissatisfied was dismal and depressing. The few who spoke with hope and satisfaction noted the meaning they were able to discern in life and work.

Many daily occurrences reported in newspapers and on television cause us to wonder what meaning life has. A guerrilla group blows up a bus, plane, or building and we wonder about the frailty and meaning of life. A sniper on a rooftop kills and wounds passerbys just as a sniper had killed a President. What is the meaning of any of these acts? In the past, senseless acts occurred; children died young; disease struck without warning. Though these occurrences were incomprehensible and absurd, individuals were not as overwhelmed and conscious of absurdity and meaninglessness.

At present, with increased social complexity and material advancement, with accelerating technological and scientific change, with economic and political confusion, many individuals question the meaning of their lives. How should life be lived if at any moment life may be extinguished by the ultimate technological advance, the nuclear bomb? Perhaps, the direction to take is one of introspection, to be self-centered and concerned with personal success, advancement, and pleasure. Perhaps, in this search for new values, the individual should only be concerned with those values which improve his own life. In the midst of the value crisis confronting our society, is it possible to discern the outline of a new revitalized values configuration? In the next two chapters, the characteristics of such a values configuration are discovered and explored.

NOTES

1. Gail Sheehy, _Passages_ (New York: E. P. Dutton & Co., Inc. 1974), p. 277.

2. This crisis is also apparent in Henry Adams' auto-biography, _The Education of Henry Adams_, ed. E. Samuels (Boston: Houghton Mifflin Co., 1974 [1918]).

3. Sheehy, _op.cit._, p. 138.

4. Alexis de Tocqueville, _Democracy in America_, G. Lawrence, trans. (Garden City, N. Y.: Doubleday Anchor, 1969 [1848]), for example, p. 155, 252-253.

5. George Grote, _A History of Greece_, vol. II (New York: Wm. L. Allison, nd), p. 263.

6. Alfred Schutz, _Collected Papers: II, Studies in Social Theory_ (The Hague: Martinus Nijhoff, 1964), p. 108.

7. _Ibid._, pp. 116-117

8. Rupert Brooke, "The Great Lover."

9. Henry Poincare, "Science and Morals" Antagonists or Allies?" trans. G. B. Halsted, _The Independent_, vol. 82 (Apr. 4, 1915), p. 39. Poincare himself takes a more moderate position between the two extremes.

10. B. F. Skinner, _Beyond Freedom and Dignity_ (New York: Bantam, 1972 [1971]), p. 1.

CHAPTER II

WHAT ARE VALUES?

In 1951, the Educational Policies Commission published a list of ten values which Americans as a whole agreed were the basic values of American society. Schools were to foster and implement these values through their teaching and educational policies. All nine subsequent values were based on the first value, the "supreme importance of the individual personality."[1] The other nine are: individual responsibility for one's own conduct; institutions are the servants of human beings; mutual consent superseding violence; the liberating effect of truth on the human mind; the fostering of excellence; human equality under the law; brotherhood; the pursuit of individual happiness without interference with or from others; spiritual enrichment.[2] Who today would still affirm that all these values should be the primary ones transmitted by school and society? Not only would few agree with this succinct list or believe that such a list in itself is sufficient to implement values education, but even fewer would agree as to the meaning of each of the stated values.

By attempting to be all things to all people, value education has little chance of success. Simultaneously, however, the acceptance and propagation of a rigid and narrow value schema condemns any value education project to failure. Though educators and parents may feel uncomfortable mandating particular values and may assume that children should choose their own values, the stipulations of some value content is necessary for both the welfare of society and of children themselves. In relation to the necessity of endorsing some value content, one author states:

> Standing quietly aside and letting youngsters
> make their own decision . . . is sometimes
> exactly the right thing to do . . . (H)owever. . .
> passivity is not to be advised as the standard
> course of action. "The parent must remember. . .
> that merely to refrain from imposing one's own
> values on the child is not to assure that he
> (the child) will develop his own. The parent
> who does not strongly endorse, even demand, the
> values he does feel are important may actually

28

be transmitting weakness of faith in all values. In attempting not to hamper the development of the child's own values, the parent may stunt the growth of any value commitment."[3]

No parent or teacher would expect that a child could learn his own language without language models and corrections or guidance where necessary. Though there is considerable experimentation in language formation, simultaneously, a language background and models provide standards by which the child can judge adequate language behavior. With values, a similar value background and value models are necessary to provide standards against which children can judge the adequacy and inadequacy of values.

In the next chapter, the content of value education is investigated in an attempt to resolve the question of which values should be taught and which values should be the content of courses in value education. In the remaining chapters of the book, the focus is reversed, being primarily concerned with the methodology for teaching values.

The use of the term "value" is often ambiguous. Each thinker discussing values and value education uses a number of different meanings, shifting from one meaning to another without any warning. This is no less a problem for educators than for philosophers, social scientists, and humanists. In his study of "the measurement of values" Rollo Handy argues that:

a marked feature of much discussion about the measurement of values is vagueness, incoherence, and confusion as to how 'value' is being used in a given inquiry. The official definitions given sometimes do not conform to what was studied, and there often appears to be little effective control over what putatively was measured.[4]

Writers of current books and articles devoted to the methods of value education have rarely considered the meaning and domain of what they are teaching or writing about. At the beginning of books on values, a very short paragraph or section defines the term "value(s)." Such definitions are often strained and lacking in clarity.

Fraenkel begins his book on how to teach about
values (not how to teach values or value conflict resolution), with the following definition(s):

A value is an idea--a concept--about what
someone thinks is important in life.[5]

Like all ideas, values do not exist in the
world of experience; they exist in people's
mind.[6]

There are a number of problems with these and other
similar definitions. At times they are not merely ambiguous, but wrong and muddled. For example, when
Fraenkel states that "values do not exist in the world
of experience; they exist in people's mind," he is
overstating his case. At times values do not merely
exist in a person's mind, but are attached to and interconnected with human experience. When someone values
a particular metal, this value is not merely an idea in
abstraction, but is interconnected within a context.
If the metal is a value because of its high price, the
individual would be mistaken to value iron greater
than gold. But if a builder were considering the value
of respective metals for a building's beams or supports,
steel would be of greater value than gold.

That there is considerable disagreement regarding
the meaning of the term "value(s)" is not only based
on a perusal of philosophic, psychological, and educational writings; but also dictionaries. The Oxford
English Dictionary devotes five columns to "value"
and three or four more to its various cognates. In a
search for a definition of value and the content of
value education, one possible way of narrowing the problem is to examine the ways to classify values. Which
classifications of value are the ones appropriate to
education?

The Domains of Values.

Before arguing that predominantly one values domain should be the concern of values education, a number of ways of classfying values domains are examined.

1. Values can be classified according to the individual or group holding the values.[7] The groups included
here may be professional groups, political groups,

30

national groups, labor unions, religious sects, ethnic groups, or even a single individual. The values considered would be dependent on the interests, preferences, desires, needs, and purposes or goals of the particular group. Physicians would have different values from executioners. For example, a recent argument has contended that a physician's values do not coincide with an executioner's values, that a physician's values would prohibit him from using his medical knowledge to be an executioner and carry out a court's death sentence. The values of an automobile factory worker would be different from those of a coal miner, a teacher, or an attorney; a Democrat's values might be different from those of a Republican. Thus, with this system of classifying values and interests, there would be an endless process of value groupings. For the purposes of value education, into which group or classification do students belong? In high school, for example, should there be groups of college-bound students and vocational students or should the division be student athletes, musicians, book-worms, actors, and politicians, with teachers in an entirely separate group? Should students be classified according to their potential, future group affiliations and interests, especially since values education would want to aim at future values and behavior as well as present?

Even if these difficulties were surmounted, another problem is apparent with this values classification. Individuals not only have unique personal values, but are members of a number of different groups. For example, the physician may also be a daughter, mother, Democrat, gourmet cook, and member of professional, religious, and social associations. Should all of a person's roles be considered or merely some of them? If only some of them, which roles should be considered most important? Finally, how are the values of one role interconnected with the values of another role?

When the focus is the values or ethical codes formulated by various professional associations and the practical ethics of various professions, this method of classification is most appropriate. However, for value education, this division or classification of the value domain does not serve our main purpose.

31

2. Values <u>can</u> be <u>classified according</u> to <u>the objects</u> <u>of value.</u> Rescher illustrated such a system through the following chart:[8]

Name of value type	Explanation of issue	Example
a. thing value	aspects of animate or inanimate objects valued.	brilliance, e.g. a gem. speed, e.g., animals, cars.
b. environmental	features or arrangements of environment	beauty of landscape. attractiveness of livroom.
c. individual or personal values	character traits, abilities, talents, i.e., features of personality life style	bravery, intelligence, cleanliness
d. group values	interactions between individuals, aspects of professional life.	respect, mutual trust
e. societal values	features of society and social life	equality under the law.

Which classification or value type is the subject matter of value education? If value education were to include all of these value types, then there has been little or no narrowing of the value domain. In truth, value education would probably include aspects or examples from each of these value types. For example, value education could include the following value discussions of each value type:

a. Thing values   Do animals have rights, e.g., the right to life?

b. Environmental values   How important is the health of human beings when compared with the need for energy and the maintenance of the economic health of a community? Under what conditions should a landscape be desecrated or ruined, e.g., is strip mining an adequate reason

	for destroying the aesthetic beauty of a landscape?
c. Individual or personal values	Are all the values which an individual could possess of equal value or is there a hierarchy of values? Should the values of human beings be given priority over the rights of animals?

Some of the value problems noted here cross into more than one values category. Thus, a course in values education could include all these categories of values and there would be no adequate narrowing of the values domain.

A classification schema could be constructed dependent on "the nature of the benefit at issue."[9] Through the following list, Rescher indicates possible value categories under this classificatory scheme:

Category of value   Sample Value

a) material-physical   health, comfort
b) economic   economic security,productiveness
c) moral   honesty, fairness
d) social   courtesy, charitableness
e) political   freedom, justice
f) aesthetic   beauty, symmetry
g) religious   piety
h) intellectual   clarity, intelligence
i) professional   success
j) sentimental   love, acceptance.[10]

It is my opinion that the value domain which must be considered by value education is (c), the moral category. This does not mean that the other categories do not enter the picture, but merely that the primary focus of value education should be in the moral or ethical category. For example, John Dewey has argued, a key stage in the resolution of any moral dilemma is its intellectualization, the recognition of the actual problem and delimiting its boundaries and features. The religious category may be included through the ideas and principles it may contribute to the resolution of a moral dilemma. Aspects of the social and political categories are not wholly removed from consideration. For example, if laws conflict with a person's moral principles or the principles of justice, political means and knowledge may assist in the reforming of the laws.

Even if the moral category is considered the main focus of value education, one might question whether an individual's life and values are really fragmented into separate categories. All value categories might be present in any values dilemma. More likely, however, one value category is dominant, depending on the context, event, need, or desire, and other values categories recede into the background. When necessary, any category can become dominant or enter into the process of values choice. When cooking, an individual is not necessarily involved with a moral dilemma. Unquestionably, if he is trying to poison an elderly, wealthy relative, the situation is predominantly moral, but under the normal circumstances of an individual cooking for himself, a group of friends, or family, the considerations may be aesthetic, social, religious, or a combination of all three. Though cooking and its relationship to these categories, the aesthetic, social and religious, may be a component of education in general, neither cooking nor these categories would be the major concern of values education.

Someone may still ask why value education should concentrate on the moral domain. Most people do not care how others furnish their home or what paintings are preferred. As a matter of personal taste, with such matters we still concur with David Hume:

> One person is more pleased with the sublime; another with the tender; a third with raillery. One has a strong sensibility to blemishes, and is extremely studious of correctness: Another has a more lively feeling of beauties, and pardons twenty absurdities and defects for one elevated or pathetic stroke. The ear of this man is entirely turned towards conciseness and energy; that man is delighted with a copious, rich, and harmonious expression. Simplicity is affected by one; ornament by another. Comedy, tragedy, satire, odes, have each its partisans, who prefer that particular species of writing to all others. It is plainly an error in a critic, to confine his approbation to one species or style of writing, and condemn

all the rest. But it is almost impossible not to feel a predilection for that which suits our particular turn and disposition. Such preferences are innocent and unavoidable, and can never reasonably be the object of dispute, because there is no standard by which they can be decided.[11]

But in the area of morals, it would be unusual for anyone to accept such relativism, such a laissez-faire attitude toward the moral principles and behavior of others. Here, it is not an unwarranted intrusion into another's private life, but concern about how the other behaves toward fellow human beings in situations involving obligation, responsibility, right and wrong, good and evil. A value, such as honesty, does not merely affect the actor's life alone. It is not merely a personal value, dependent on personal taste, but a value which affects others. Furthermore, the repercussions of dishonesty can be great, not merely affecting a single relationship, but affecting the social fibre as a whole. Though the United States is relatively a permissive society and though society might not want to dictate which moral principles are accepted, neither society nor schools can ignore this component of education. Variety or pluralism might be wholly tolerable in morality as well as other aspects of human life, but such pluralism has its limitations and boundaries.

With these ideas in mind, I intend to stress the domain of values known as ethics or morality.

In the Lifeline program for values education curriculum, the authors use "moral education" throughout their book to mean "education in and about values."[12] One of their reasons for assuming that moral education includes "the total personality and social structure,"[13] is the response they received from adolescents about times when they admired adults:

> Adults were often commended as helpful,
> as treating a teenager well, when they
> were quietly efficient in teaching,
> handling an awkward situation, organi-
> zing work or a party, coping with
> changing a wheel on the car, righting
> a capsized dinghy and so on.[14]

Here, of course, is the assertion that an adult, whether professional teacher or not, most effectively teaches, transmits, or motivates values and values development if that person is admired and respected by adolescents.[15] Fundamental to all moral education is the environment in which the child or adolescent interacts. That environment is not dependent on physical objects, but on social interactions with adults.

The second example is of food marketing with a child. The child asks his parents to buy all sorts of items, some seen on television, some alluringly, colorfully packaged, and others friends have praised. Obviously, most parents cannot purchase all the things a child would like. Even if it were possible to buy everything, most parents would question the wisdom of such a course. One way for parents to cope with this problem is the following: Allow the child to spend a certain amount of money on the food he desires, perhaps stipulating that the food actually must be eaten. The child might be told in advance of the shopping trip, how much he is allowed to spend and then given the tools for determining what can be bought for his money. Such tools might include a study of the weekly food pages of the local paper and discussion with parents of the relative merit of alternative choices. Another method might be for the parent to make a shopping list of the foods and other household supplies to be bought each week. This would be done in consultation with the family. Organized meal and snack planning would avoid a child's emotional emphasis on snack food. A child might even decide that it is cheaper and more fun to make his own snacks. How does this example relate to moral education, since it would be impossible to call these choices "moral judgments"? Many of the same elements enter into the process of making decisions regarding food purchases as are required for moral judgments. This is especially true for the child who does not possess the cognitive abilities, experience, and problem solving techniques that an older person would possess. For example, in making a moral judgment an individual must ascertain which facts relate to the moral dilemma. With food purchasing, appropriate facts are also relevant, e.g., which items are on special sale? Cook books might be studied to ascertain what foods are needed for particular recipes. The child also becomes aware of all the variables a parent takes into consideration when food shopping, even if the parent almost unconsciously makes these judgments. What staples, paper goods, and soaps are needed might cause the child to recognize the value of conservation, realizing that with conservation of paper goods, for instance, other food items can be bought.

Furthermore, and probably most important for the purposes of value education, the child must construct some type of hierarchy regarding the items of most value to him. He might consider which items he likes best, which last longest, what television commercials have claimed, etc. Finally, he judges one item to be more worthwhile than another. When asked to make value judgments concerning the relative value of different supermarket items, the child begins to realize that there are different levels of importance, and that an individual does not begin to evaluate and judge without prior experience. Evaluation takes place throughout life. By having the child evaluate the relative worth of various market items, evaluation becomes a self-conscious activity and not merely something done haphazardly. Then, whenever the child is faced with a moral or ethical problem, the same self-conscious judgmental procedure may take place.

What does the term "value" mean?

A search for a definition of the term "value" or of any of its cognates reveals that instead of one single agreed upon definition, a great variety of definitions exist. This is because the meaning of the term "value" is not fixed but varies according to the demands or needs of a particular philosophical, psychological, sociological, or educational theory or study. Some aspects of this variation in meaning are worth noting.

1. Subjectivity versus objectivity.

    a) John wants to buy a new car.
    b) The child wants a lollipop.
    c) The Monet "Water Lily" paintings at L'Orangerie pleased me.
    d) Mr. Smith cares a great deal about the preservation of historic buildings and monuments.

Are all of the above value statements merely an expression of the desires, feelings, cares, tastes, and hopes of a human agent? Are values in general wholly subjective in that they are entirely based on the individual human beings. Or are values based on something or some quality intrinsic to the object, state of affairs, or situation? In other words, are values objective or subjective?

Both ways of defining values have been popular since the beginning of the conscious development of values theories during the nineteenth century. However, the subjective approach seems most popular today. Psychologists and educational theorists have strengthened the subjective orientation. If one considers some of the basic ideas of leading psychological theories, this popularity is understandable.

Association or classical conditioning learning theories assume that the human agent is motivated to pursue some goal. This goal orientation assumes that the individual's subjective, personal values motivate behavior. The individual pursues a particular goal or acts in a particular manner to achieve a goal because he deems the goal to be of value. Since human needs and the previous learning and experiences of the individual determine his motivating forces and his presently desired goals, the values are based on the individual self--the person's own desires and feelings regarding objects, experiences, events, and states of affairs. For example, one psychologist, Thurstone, discussed the subjectivity of values as an introduction to the problem of values measurement:

> Human values are essentially subjective. They can certainly not be adequately represented by physical objects. Their intensities or magnitudes cannot be represented by physical measurement. At the very start we are faced with the problem of establishing a subjective metric. This is the central theme in modern psychophysics in its many applications to the measurement of social values, moral values, and esthetic values. Exactly the same problem reappears in the measurement of utility in economics.[16]

Understandably, Thurstone's measurement grid follows his assertion of the subjectivity of values in that he uses qualities possessed by the object, but stresses subjective desiring.

Less popular at the present time is the view that values are objective; that is, intrinsic or inherent to objects, states of affairs, or experiences themselves. If the world and everything in the world were created by a Divine Being, then things themselves would possess value. This value would exist inherently in objects, whether or not human beings valued these objects or even knew of their existence.

Both theories--subjective and objective--have been criticized. If values are wholly subjective, is the ethical world nothing but a mire of chaos with no agreement at all on ethical behavior or judgments? Does a television soap opera share the same value as "Hamlet"? Are human beings really the measure of all things with each individual liking or desiring different values? If a subjective definition of value is accepted, is any agreement possible between individuals and societies?

On the topic of objective orientation, matters are not much better. If there were objectivity of values, one might question why all individuals do not adhere to the same values. Why has it been impossible, to date, to discover the objective moral law to which all human beings are willing to adhere? If a Divine Being does govern all things, why is there evil? Why should a good or benign Divine Being allow the existence of evil?

2. Value: <u>A</u> <u>Noun</u> <u>and</u> <u>a</u> <u>Verb</u>.

Webster's <u>Unabridged</u> <u>Dictionary</u> and the <u>Oxford</u> <u>English</u> <u>Dictionary</u> both note definitions of value, a noun, and value, a verb. Let's look at two statements to see this difference.

a) Gold has considerable value on world commodity exchanges.

b) I value her friendship above my life.

In the first instance, when speaking of gold as a value, "value" functions as a noun, indicating an objective value. In the second statement, "value" is a verb, indicating my judgment of a particular relationship.

John Dewey has pointed to the two sides of the value coin. On one side, value, the noun, can refer to the thing subjectively desired or the objective quality inherent in a thing; but in the verb form, it serves to indicate a conscious judgment. Dewey's interests favored value as a verb, as the outcome of a judgmental process. Basically, Dewey claimed that it is necessary to abandon the subjective--objective dichotomy and to seek an alternative to resolve the stalemate between the two. It has been suggested that merely feeling or desiring something means little. The important idea, bridging the objective and subjective, is the "betweenness", the evaluation of the object, state of affairs, or experience, by the subject, the human agent. There are many things that individuals fleetingly desire and yet shun. This is not merely thoughtless willpower shunning the forbidden, but rather, according to Dewey, the individual evaluates the worth or value of the object in relation to quite a number of elements such as the consequences of his choice, the means necessary to obtain the desired object, his past overt or vicarious experiences, and the views of others. Therefore, when Dewey presents his theory of value he is actually presenting a "theory of valuation."

This exceptionally individualistic and subjective orientation occurs in other psychologies such as the humanistic psychology of Carl Rogers. The individual constructs his own future through his choices. As he makes choices and determines or develops his own self, the values he accepts evolve. Here, too, value choice is a subjective matter, based on the feelings, desires, and choices of each individual. Carl Rogers expresses these views when discussing his non-directive psychological counseling technique:

> Non-directive counseling is based on the
> assumption that the client has the right
> to select his own life goals, even though
> these may be at variance with the goals
> that the counselor might choose for him.
> There is also the belief that if the in-
> dividual has a modicum of insight into
> himself and his problems, he will be like-
> ly to make this choice wisely.[17]

When Rogers discusses values, he uses the cognate "valuing" saying that "valuing is the tendency of a person to show preference."[18] Thus, following his non-directive counseling theory, Rogers indicates that valuing is the means by which the individual selects and creates his own life and values. Of course, these theorists, whether associationist or humanist, accept the notion that more than one individual may desire the same object or may place value, high or low, on identical things, situations, experience, or states of affairs.

What this discussion has accentuated is the difficulty of defining the term "value(s)," since definitions are embedded within larger theories. In later chapter when psychological theories and methods of value education are discussed the problem of meaning will surface again.

NOTES

1. Educational Policies Commission, Moral and Spiritual Values in the Public Schools (Washington, D.C.: NEA, 1951), p. 18.

2. Ibid., pp. 19-29.

3. Dorothy Barclay, "Values for Children--Who Sets Them" New York Times, August 11, 1957. In Garry Wills, ed., Values Americans Live by (New York: Arno Press, 1974), p. 199.

4. Rollo Handy, The Measurement of Values (St. Louis, Mo.: Warren H. Greene, Inc., 1970), p. 207, cf. p. 43.

5. Jack R. Fraenkel, How to Teach about Values: An Analytic Approach (Englewood Cliffs, N.J.: Prentice-Hall, Inc., 1977), p. 6.

6. Ibid., p. 7.

7. Nicholas Rescher, Introduction to Value Theory (Englewood Cliffs, N. J.: Prentice-Hall, Inc., 1969), p. 14.

8. Ibid., pp. 14-15.

9. Ibid., p. 16.

10. Ibid.

11. David Hume, "Of the Standard of Taste," Essays, Moral, Political, and Literary by David Hume, T. H. Greene and T. H. Grose, eds. (Darmstadt: Scietia Verlag Aalen, 1964 1882), p. 281.

12. Peter McPhail, J. R. Ungoed-Thomas, Hilary Chapman, Learning to Care (Niles, Ill.: Argus Communication, 1975), p. viii.

13. Ibid.

14. Peter McPhail, J. R. Ungoed-Thomas, Hilary Chapman, Moral Education in the Secondary School (London: Longman, 1972), p. 33.

15. McPhail, _et.al._, Learning to Care, pp. 9-10.

16. Handy, _op.cit._, p. 6. Quoted from L. L.
    Thurstone, "The Measurement of Values,"
    Psychological Review, vol. 61 (1954), p. 47.

17. Carl R. Rogers, _Counseling and Psychotherapy_
    (Boston: Houghton Mifflin Co., 1942), pp. 126-127.

18. _Ibid_.

CHAPTER III

WHICH VALUES SHOULD BE TRANSMITTED?

Values for the Good Life and a Democratic Society.

1. The One and the Many.

     Human life and the history of ideas has been a
continuing battle between the one and the many. At
the outset of Against the Current, Isaiah Berlin describes the fundamental tenets of those who search for
the one. They believed:

> that human nature was fundamentally the same
> in all times and places; that local and his-
> torical variations were unimportant compared
> with the constant central core in terms of
> which human beings could be defined as a
> species . . .; that there were universal
> human goals; that a logically connected
> structure of laws and generalizations sus-
> ceptible to demonstration and verification
> could be constructed and replace the chaotic
> amalgam of ignorance, mental laziness,
> guesswork, superstition, prejudice, dogma,
> (and) fantasy.[1]

At all times and in all places, the dominant forces
guiding human life and catalyzing thought and behavior have supported the belief that eventually
heaven would be achieved on earth. Over the years,
thinkers have created utopias which could be achieved
only if human beings followed the right path--one
single road to the promised land. Though there were
many theories and arguments regarding which one truth,
one way, or one method would provide a panacea to the
perfect and happy life, there was no doubt that the
one way existed. Out of the confusion and chaos of
ignorance and unhappiness would emerge a reborn human
being and society, reborn because of the acceptance
of the one way. Various authorities pointed to their
own single answer. God or gods, religions and
religious leaders, philosophers and political leaders,
dictators and pacifists, scientists and poets all had
a version, a vision of the one way. Politicians and
philosophers alike, however, have feared this

44

concentration on one way or one authority. For example, Benjamin Franklin believed the acceptance of one way to be a human frailty. He states that "most men, indeed, as well as most sects in religion think themselves in possession of all truth, and that whatever others differ from them it is so far error."[2] Franklin also quotes a French lady who takes such a view of one correct value system to its ultimate, logical extreme: "I don't know how it happens,. . . but I meet with nobody but myself that is always in the right."[3]

The philosopher, John Herman Randall, Jr. castigates the acceptance of and devotion to absolute political principles when he states:

> Surely there are more political principles
> in active circulation today than for many
> a long year. One has only to open the morn-
> ing paper to be caught in a barrage of them.
> They volley from the Right, they thunder
> from the Left; and even peaceable citizens,
> anxious to go about their business undisturb-
> ed in the broad Center, have had to lay in
> a generous stock in self-defense. When we
> look across the seas we find the atmosphere
> from Moscow to Madrid so cluttered up with
> eternal principles in irresponsible conflict
> that it is hard to discern any merely human
> beings. . .
>
> Side by side with this strife of principles
> has gone a marked decline in what we used
> to regard as political intelligence.[4]

Though Randall wrote this in 1938 at the beginning of the Second World War, his comments about strife between ultimate principles guaranteeing the good life are just as appropriate today.

Throughout the ages, many people have held the view that there are pluralistic, equally valid, value systems. Anthropologists have described how different societies, cultures, and tribes extolled different values and art, celebrated different holidays, accepted different modes of behavior, and enforced different customs and taboos. Historians have often noted the different interests, preferences, needs, national experiences and loyalties, and the different social

45

forces and political beliefs of different countries. From the travels of Herodotus and Marco Polo, world travelers have brought back to their native lands stories about what they characterized as strange or exotic customs and mores. Travelers were surprised to learn that fantastic customs and unusual forms of behavior were normal and even required in some societies.

Isaiah Berlin analyzes the ideas of the previously ignored thinkers who accepted value pluralism. Those thinkers argued that human beings and societies actually accept many different values and moral codes instead of one single unified principle and vision. Furthermore, there would be no way of deciding between these different contending systems. Berlin describes these thinkers as believing:

> that beliefs involving value-judgment, and the institutions founded upon them, rested not on discoveries of objective and unalter- able natural facts, but on human opinion, which was variable and different between societies and at different times; that moral and political values, and in particular just- ice and social arrangements in general, rested on fluctuating human convention. . . It seemed to follow that no universal truths, establish- ed by scientific methods, that is, truths that anyone could verify by the use of proper methods, anywhere, at any time, could in principle be established in human affairs.[5]

David Hume speaks in a similar manner when commenting upon the different moral sentiments accepted by differ- ent people with even son and father embracing different moral principles and systems.[6] In matters of taste and value standards, Hume argued that there was no way of deciding between differing views. Even in matters of taste, however, the generosity of spirit which would allow for the absence of dispute, which Hume so de- sired, often has seemed absent. In any case, it is difficult to argue that a plurality of tastes would endanger the survival of a society. Extreme pluralism in morality, however, has its dangers and difficulties. Individuals could give their allegiance to any beliefs or opinions no matter how radical or reactionary. The ultimate choice might rest on a person's unexamined

feelings and emotions, not on any rational warrant.
If people were insulated in their own sets of beliefs,
it might prove difficult, if not impossible, to com-
prehend the beliefs of other individuals and groups.
Even the act of meaningful communication might prove
a futile exercise, for if each person meant different
things when using key value concepts such as justice,
democracy, and goodness, conversations about such
matters would not be meaningful dialogues about mutual-
ly understood subjects and interests. One might wonder
whether a world structured of such value pluralism
could ever be anything but anarchy or a battlefield of
competing values.

The history of the American experience in many
ways reflects the competition and battle between the
one and the many. Let us look at two examples to see
how the one and the many have been in conflict in
American society and then, to see whether these conflicts have been resolved.

The one and the many in government and political
life. The founding fathers were fearful of the powers
of a centralized government, an absolute authority.
The 1776 Articles of Confederation asserted that each
of the thirteen states would retain its "sovereignty,
freedom and independence," with the confederation described as a "firm league of friendship." Even though
historians have described this as "a long step toward
a true Union,"[7] there was considerable conflict before
and after the ratification of these articles. Many
leaders expressed strong reservations against any close
union between the colonies. Though Benjamin Franklin
later embraced the principles and ideals of the American Constitution, he had earlier questioned the merits
of a strong central government when he said:

I cannot but apprehend more mischief than
benefit from a closer union . . . .
Here numberless and needless places, enormous
salaries, pensions, perquisites, bribes,
groundless quarrels, foolish expeditions,
false accounts or no accounts, contracts and
jobs devour all revenue, and produce continual
necessity in the midst of natural plenty. I
apprehend, therefore, that to unite us intim-
ately will only be to corrupt and poison us
also.[8]

John Adams also notes how the debates of the Continental Congress were really disagreements concerning the one and the many. For example, Patrick Henry sided with the belief in one Nation. He states:

> The distinction between Virginians, Pennsylvanians, New Yorkers and New Englanders are no more. I am not a Virginian, but an American. . . .
>
> All America is thrown into one mass.[9]

In general, small colonies were afraid larger colonies would assume power. People were afraid that their freedoms and rights might be lost if a powerful, centralized government were created. Plebians feared that a wealthy, land-owning minority might become a self-perpetuating, hereditary aristocracy. In other words, what was feared was the vision of the one, a simple, ultimate truth and power. Simultaneously, however, others feared the inherent weakness and insecurity of anarchy, pluralism, and thus, a loose federation of "friendship," in which ultimate power and authority rested with the separate colonies. This conflict between the one and the many was only one of a series of conflicts at this time. For example, in 1783 there was an attempted military coup within the American colonies in which segments of the Colonial Army desired to wrest power and install a military dictatorship. It was Washington who argued against such a dictatorship and in favor of a republican government.[10]

The conflict between the one and the many was finally resolved not with the victory of one of these two alternative extremes, but with the acceptance of both as necessary, complimentary, interdependent elements in human life and in government. The Constitution recognized the need for a central government and for the maintenance of individual state's rights, the validity and necessity of a leader, an elected President whose power would be checked by two other branches of government.

The One and the Many in Social Life.

The title of Israel Zangwell's play, "The Melting Pot," quickly fired the imagination of Americans and became the fashionable slogan for describing the Americanization of millions of immigrants. To be an American meant the acceptance of the basic values of an

48

American. If one's own cultural values were retained
in any form, they were hidden within one's own private
life. For example, though it was acceptable to enjoy
the cooking of one's homeland and to continue to cele-
brate one's national and religious holidays, American
values, modes of behavior, and beliefs had to be manifested in public life. Though politicians and educators extolled the importance of minority groups, this
seemed to be no more than lip-service to the different
groups making up American society. Maurice Davie
argued that minority values and customs have dissolved
in the face of mainstream American values, when he
states:

> Modification of the culture of minority groups
> toward the pattern of the dominant group . . .
> appears inevitable, at least in any environment
> such as is provided by the United States . . .
> In the conflict of different cultures that
> arises in a composite society, the culture
> of the dominant group prevails, not merely
> because of force of numbers but because it
> represents for the individual a better ad-
> justment to the life-conditions of the society
> in question.[11]

> . . . there appear to be on the one hand
> centripetal forces at work to maintain and
> perpetuate minority differences, and on the
> other hand centrifugal forces operating to
> dissolve them. In this struggle, the dis-
> integrating forces represented by the domin-
> ant American pattern tends to prevail . . .
> The trend is inevitable. It is simply a
> question of how fast it proceeds.[12]

If someone were poor or unemployed, uneducated or unable to speak English, his condition was blamed on his
own unwillingness or inability to integrate within the
mainstream of American life. That mainstream, it was
asserted, was always there for anyone who accepted
American values and lived and worked in accordance
with the Puritan work ethic.

Nineteenth-century and early twentieth-century
novels extolled the virtues of American values. For
example, in Oliver Optic's Little by Little or The
Cruise of the Flyaway, the following description of

success is given:

> Little by little, Paul Duncan had worked
> his way up . . . to the command of one of
> the finest ocean steamers that sailed out
> of New York. He was exceedingly popular
> with the public, and was often quoted as
> the noblest specimen of a gallant captain
> . . . . He is not rich, as wealth is
> measured in our day, though he has some
> property, and receives a liberal salary
> from the Steamship Company; but in the
> higher and truer sense, he is rich--rich
> in possession of a noble and lofty char-
> acter, and a faith which reaches beyond
> the treasures of this world . . . .
>
> Now, reader, if you like the character
> of Paul Duncan, build up one like it. Be
> true to yourself, to your parents, and to
> your God; be patient and perservering, and
> you will obtain your full measure of suc-
> cess, though like him you are obliged to
> win it Little by Little.[13]

Horatio Alger's story, The Erie Train Boy, also stressed similar American values. The streets of America
were paved with gold, but only for those who accepted
Americanization. Though this seemed to be generally
accepted, many flaws appeared in the melting pot, the
American success myth. Writers, such as John Steinbeck
stirringly and emotionally wrote of the poor, the less
fortunate, the downtrodden, and persecuted, those hidden millions who had never experienced the American
dream and were alienated from the American mainstream.[14]

Even the middle class, which was the personifica-
tion of the American dream, did not seem to possess the
good life. Sociological studies of American towns revealed this tragic, if not fatal, flaw. For example,
Lynd and Lynd in Middletown described a town and a way
of life with the following characteristics:

> Its wealth has greatly increased. Its in-
> habitants have more things in their houses,
> better clothes on their backs and more means
> of amusement, and its health is decidedly
> better. But it gets less fun out of its

job, its home life has pretty well gone
to pot, it is inefficiently and often
corruptly governed, and its ideas and
habits are almost as regimented as those
of a South Sea Islander under the taboo
system. The individualism with which we
endow the older generations is disappear-
ing.[15]

Was this the consequence of the melting pot? Did as-
similation cause the conditions Lynd and Lynd describe?
Is this what an American's life must become if he
wants to achieve within American society?

   Throughout the early emphasis on Americanization
and the melting pot, the advantages of the Puritan
work ethic and the land of opportunity, and the possibility of success and upward socio-economic mobility
for all, there was still some recognition of diversity
and pluralism.[16]   America showed that it was proud of
the various nationalities that contributed to its history, growth, and culture. If anything, such cultural,
social, religious, and political pluralism was seen as
foundational to American democracy. Peter Steinfels
claims: "The class of groups in the pluralist model
took place within a consensus about the rules of the
game and the fundamental values that sustained these
rules."[17] What allowed such a pluralistic clash of
ethnic, religious, and social groups to vie democratic-
ally for their various interests?

   America had been particularly blessed . . .
   Lockian liberalism had encountered vir-
   tually no challengers as the framework
   for American politics. No established
   aristocracy provided the economic and
   social base for resisting the democratic
   and egalitarian current of the nineteenth
   century. Aided by the safety valves of
   size and wealth, and by its remarkable
   political institutions, including the two
   party system, the new society had developed a gift for compromise and pragmatic
   adaptation.[18]

The "compromise and pragmatic adaptation" of various
groups within the political system also seemed to
characterize all other segments of American social and

political life. John Dewey's optimistic and rational book, <u>Democracy</u> <u>and</u> <u>Education</u>, extolled the use of experimentation and rational thought to affect compromise and harmony within the school and classroom. Children so educated would become the basis of a new America.

The rumblings of unrest, however, already existed. Finally, during the '60s, such discomfort with the American answer to the opposing forms of the one and the many, the melting-pot and political pluralism, erupted and caused a rise in the doctrine of the many. Blacks, various ethnic and religious groups all claimed a right to pursue their own values and heritage. The poor, students, women, the elderly, handicapped, and gifted also claimed they had been deprived of rights and the unique opportunities promised to all Americans. In other words, numerous groups claimed they had been cheated, that the American dream had not worked, that the melting pot had merely been a myth, which in reality had caused them to lose values which were truly important. In order to become part of the mainstream and experience American success, especially material success, people had felt compelled to reject much which contributed to meaningful, interpersonal relationships and much of what they inherited from their own unique, historic past. People spoke of themselves as part of a "rat race," immersed in a competitive world which disintegrated the cooperative spirit of smaller communities of bygone days.

These are the thoughts of those who have criticized the melting-pot social policy and extolled ethnic identity. Writing of the American Irish, Andrew Greeley expressed his anger in the following paradox:

> I am saying to American society, "You've tried to turn us into lower-middle class WASPS and, damn it all, you haven't succeeded." On the other hand, I am saying to the American Irish, "Why did you let them turn you into lower-middle class WASPS?"[19]

Michael Novak expresses his frustration with the Polish American experience of the melting pot:

> What price is exacted by America when . . .
> it sucks other cultures of the world
> and processes them? What do people have

> to lose before they can qualify as true
> Americans?
>
> For one thing, a lot of blue stars--and
> silver and gold ones--must hang in the
> window. You proved you loved America.. by
> dying for it in its wars . . .
>
> I don't have other figures at hand. But
> when the Poles were only four percent of
> the population (in 1917-19) they account-
> ed for twelve percent of the nation's
> casualties in World War I . . .
>
> There is . . . a blood test. "Die for
> us and we'll give you a chance."[20]

Similar anger with and reservations about the American
dream were expressed by numerous other authors. Was
there an alternative? Was there another way? It has
been argued that no matter one's national origin, race,
sex, or religion, a person has a right to the goods
America offers without giving up roots, national heritage, or original values. From 1960 to the present
day, this country has witnessed a rise in interest in
cultural pluralism and ethnic groups demanding American
success without concomitant Americanization. Recent
conflicts among groups often have not seemed resolvable
according to older formulae and traditional game rules.
With each new demand for equality, equal opportunity,
and rights, there has been a backlash from some other
group. Often such demands left the perspective of group
interests and ethnicity and became rampant, egotistical
individualism, the "me-ism" of the 1970s. Again, there
has been conflict between the one and the many. Though
each group or each person seemed to advocate some one
single set of values in the context of the entire society, there appeared to be many value systems vying
against each other.

The problem for value and moral education is which
values and moral principles are necessary to foster and
catalyze moral development within a democratic society?[21]
Answers to this question have generally been avoided by
theorists writing about value or moral education. In
the context of the extreme cultural and value pluralism
of American democracy, few would dare suggest that there
is a unified system or set of values or a moral code
which every person should accept. Even parents are not

certain which values and moral rules are appropriate
and valid for their own children. By avoiding answers
to the questions of which values and moral principles
foster moral development and the good life, educators,
parents, and adults in general often have accepted an
anarchic, extremely relativistic position. They seem
to have tacitly accepted the notion that all moral principles and values are of equal worth for twentieth century American society. This is not true! A multitude
of values have been embraced and tolerated without the
realization that a society, community, or nation cannot survive without some cohesive, integrated bonds,
without certain basic values commonly shared. Thus,
if the United States is to remain a pluralistic society
in which many diverse ethnic, religious, and cultural
groups live in harmony, there must simultaneously be
the acceptance of certain fundamental values. Only
with a harmonious balance between the one and the many
can American society continue and flourish.

Before discussing which values and moral principles
foster moral development, two qualifications are necessary. First, a complete set of character traits, moral
rules, or values is not being offered. My only concern
here is with those basic values, character traits, or
moral principles which foster the moral development of
the individual and society. Second, only a sketch of
such character traits, moral rules and values can be
presented here since a wholly satisfactory analysis and
presentation would be far longer than is possible in
this short section.

At least four categories of values are needed for
moral development, a) facilitating values; b) contextual values; c) basic moral principles; and d) character
or personal traits. Although many values overlap these
categories, it is advantageous to look at each of these
broad value categories separately and see which specific values could be included in each.

a) Facilitating Values

Facilitating values refer to those values which
are necessary for any discussion and resolution of
moral conflicts or dilemmas. In judicial courts, such
facilitating values would be called legal procedures to
be distinguished from the laws forbidding certain behavior. Though there often are laws concerning legal

procedure, such laws do not usually determine court or jury decisions. However, in the belief that just and fair procedure is as important as the guilt or innocence of a defendant, any infraction of the mandated procedure can be grounds for the dismissal of the case. Without facilitating values, value judgments and choices would be as impossible as a court case without any judicial procedure.

The following values or "dispositions" as William K. Frankena calls them, are among those facilitating values necessary for values discussions and education: "clarity, consistency, rigor of thought, concern for semantic meaningfulness, methodological awareness, (and) consciousness of assumptions."[22] Of course, other facilitating values can be produced, e.g., the willingness to give reasons for value judgments and the ability to judge some reasons more valid than others. Though it is impossible to analyze all facilitating values here, at least a number of points can be clarified:

(i) While Frankena calls these values "dispositions," other writers refer to them as "habits." Instead of being external and consciously applied, cognitive qualities should become habits in that they should often be used without conscious thought.

(ii) Children do not come to value discussions possessing mature facilitating values. One of the goals of value education must be the development of mature habits of thought, for only through such procedural maturity can an individual successfully confront and resolve the complex value dilemmas of this century.

(iii) Though the values mentioned here are necessary for any cognitive judgment, their importance for value judgments cannot be underestimated. Without any argument, it would be agreed that subjects like mathematics and science require these facilitating values. When turning to personal values, many individuals seem to think that emotional choice or desire is sufficient. Unfortunately, values chosen emotionally often are illusions. After experiencing such emotionally chosen values, there is often regret and sorrow. Facilitating values are the procedural tools which allow for rational value choice and foresight.

b) Contextual Values.

Contextual values designate the quality of the environment most conducive to moral development. Most often, educators and parents consider the character of the moral dilemmas presented to students, the method by which to catalyze thought and questioning, and the quality of the interpersonal relationships, between adult and student, and between student and student. The setting, or context, is more often ignored. Though moral development can and does take place in numerous contexts, moral development can prove more successful within a context particularly suitable for such education. No school, society, or family can expect its students and children to possess values, moral principles, and character traits which do not occur within the educational and social context. This assumption is understandable if there is agreement that the school, society, and family must actually manifest accepted moral principles and character traits in practice prior to their acceptance by children. Paul H. Hirst stresses the role of the moral character of schools in facilitating a child's moral education:

> ...there is the simple fact that, quite apart from its specific educational functions, the life of the school should in all respects be morally acceptable. In the relations between children, between children and adults, between the head of the school and the staff, there should be patterns of behavior that are justifiable in general terms. Bullying, dishonesty, decisions based on personal convenience, the pointless maintenance of traditions, the irrelevant use of status, all of these are indefensible in any institution, and certainly in one which is expressly concerned with moral affairs. If those running the schools do not maintain a morally justifiable institution, why should pupils take seriously their explicit moral posturings?[23]

Though schools, administrators and teachers assert the need for moral education, too frequently this has very limited meaning and is inconsistent with the actual school climate and structure. Amitai Etzioni forcefully illustrates how the "schools' moral climate" often contradicts education for value or moral reasoning. For example, the distribution of grades often reflects group or program placement; student trustees

56

or monitors can make "unsavory trade(s)" of privileges; sports are no longer aimed at character formation or sportsmanship, but winning no matter how.[24] In addition, "ethical misconduct is explained and 'plea-bargained' away in private and seldom used for educational opportunity." Etzioni asserts that schools should examine "the value it communicates so effectively in its total arrangement."[25]

In _A Theory of Justice,_ John Rawls argues that an individual develops a sense of justice and fairness if first he is nurtured in a loving home and then becomes part of an association with a just social arrangement:

> this person develops ties of friendly
> feeling and trust toward others in the
> association as they with evident inten-
> tion comply with their duties and obli-
> gations and live up to the ideals of
> their station.[26]

Given the just arrangement of an association such as a school, and the guarantee that all members of the association have appropriate roles, moral development proceeds in the following way:

> the evident intention to honor one's
> obligations and duties is seen as a
> form of good will, and this recogni-
> tion arouses feelings of friendship
> and trust in return. In due course
> the reciprocal effects of everyone's
> doing his share strengthen one another
> until a kind of equilibrium is reached.
> But we may also suppose that the newer
> members of the association recognize
> moral exemplars, that is, persons who
> are in various ways admired and who ex-
> hibit to a high degree the ideal cor-
> responding to their position.[27]

No list or analysis of contextual values is offered here for it is assumed that any educational association must accept and manifest whichever values it attempts to transmit to children or adolescents. Some of these values are noted in the next two sections.

c) <u>Moral</u> <u>Principles</u>.

Basic moral principles are those required for the maintenance of a democratic society, social harmony, individual fulfillment, and personal autonomy. The following are included as basic moral principles: the rights and worth of individuals, principles of justice and fairness, the acceptance of principles of equal opportunity, equality, and freedom. Actually, these represent concepts which have become part of the history of moral and ethical theory, and because of the complexity of their conceptualization these basic moral principles cannot be carefully discussed here. Instead, one concept shall be emphasized which is of fundamental importance, that of respect for persons.

John Rawls defines self-respect first as including:

> a person's sense of his own value, his secure conviction that his conception of his good, his plan of life, is worth carrying out. And second, self-respect implies a confidence in one's ability . . . to fulfill one's intention.[28]

Though Rawls stresses respect in terms of how an individual feels about himself, the development and maintenance of self-respect are inextricably tied to society and other individuals. Thus, the individual cannot wholly control whether he or she possesses self-respect. Rather, the character of social interactions, the relationship with family and friends, the role a person has in society, school, and the community, the possibility of fulfilling dreams and hopes, all contribute to the degree a person achieves self-respect.

I once knew a high school student who wrote a poignant composition about the value that education should have for an individual. This student said that without a high school education, a person is nothing; without a college education a person is nothing. Only an education would allow him to achieve his life's desires and hopes. What was it that he wanted? He wanted: a wife and children, a small home of his own, a job, and maybe, someday, he said, "I would like to take a vacation." He continued by noting that only with these basics could he be a person.

What were his chances of achieving any of these
basics? In his young life, he had been transferred
from one foster home to another, twelve in all. He
had a continuous record of school failure, was labelled
a "trouble-maker" by school authorities, was disliked
and even feared by his peers, had no hobbies, and did
not take part in extra-curricula activities. In every
area where it was possible for a human being to achieve
self-respect, family, school, and friends, this student
had failed. He was not respected and didnot respect
himself. If a person is to achieve self-respect, others
must respect him. These others include family, school,
social organizations, and community. Such respect is
due another human being not because that person is intelligent, talented, attractive, creative, or competent,
but merely by virtue of being a human being.

d) <u>Character</u> <u>or</u> <u>Personal</u> <u>Virtues</u>.

Though character virtues, such as honesty, are not
prominent in contemporary moral philosophy or psychology,
I believe that certain events indicate a renewed interest in them. The following are some of the many character virtues worthwhile for human beings to possess:
honesty, trustworthiness, impartiality, consideration
of others, and conscientiousness. Certain other virtues
are rarely mentioned today. Though courage seems to
have become an archaic quality, I would like to rein-
state it. As Socrates asserted in the <u>Laches</u>, courage
is not a quality which is only displayed on the battlefield. Socrates includes in his class of courageous
people those who are courageous in the face of disease,
poverty, in public affairs, those who withstand pain
and fear, and those who control themselves against excessive desires and pleasures.[29] Included here would
be individuals who have the courage of their covictions,
are willing to stand up for their values, and be responsible for their principles and actions.

Personal virtues are those qualities which determine how the individual lives a moral life and makes
moral decisions. Included here would be characteristics such as imagination, creativity, persistence, commitment, fidelity, and authenticity.[30] For example,
though the quality "creativity" is usually linked with
artistic creation and scientific discovery, its inclusion here in a discussion of moral values is appropriate. If values are not dispensed in carefully

controlled doses and learned through rote, memorization or indoctrination, then the individual must use some degree of creativity in resolving unique and different moral dilemmas.

In summation, members of a pluralistic society should not care how someone eats, the fashions preferred, the books read, the hobbies enjoyed, the sports played, whether one is an introvert or extrovert, serious or humorous. However, there must be great concern about the quality of an individual's moral life. If a person asserts preference for being a liar, a bigot, or an amoralist, then society has a right to be concerned and reproach that person.

NOTES

1. Isaiah Berlin, <u>Against</u> <u>the</u> <u>Current</u> (New York: Viking Press, 1979) p. 1.

2. Henry Steele Commager and Allan Nevins, eds. <u>The</u> <u>Heritage</u> <u>of</u> <u>America</u> (Boston: Little, Brown & Co., 1939), p. 200.

3. <u>Ibid.</u>

4. John Herman Randall, Jr., "On the Importance of Being Unprincipled," <u>The</u> <u>American</u> <u>Scholar</u> <u>Reader</u>, H. Hayden and B. Saunders, eds. (New York: Atheneum Publishers, 1960), p. 73.

5. Berlin, <u>op</u>.<u>cit</u>., p. 2.

6. David Hume, "Of the Standard of Taste," <u>Essays</u>, <u>Moral</u>, <u>Political</u>, and <u>Literary</u> by David Hume, T. H. Greene and T. H. Grose, eds. (Darmstadt: Scietia Verlag Aalen, 1964 1882), p. 283.

7. Commager and Nevins, <u>op</u>.<u>cit</u>., p. 191.

8. Henry Steele Commager and Richard B. Morris, <u>The</u> <u>Spirit</u> <u>of</u> '<u>Seventy-Six</u> (New York: Harper & Row Publ., 1958), p. 55. Quoted from Albert Henry Smyth, ed. <u>The</u> <u>Writings</u> <u>of</u> <u>Benjamin</u> <u>Franklin</u>, vol. VI (New York: Macmillan Co., 1905-1907), pp.311-312.

9. Commager and Morris, <u>op</u>.<u>cit</u>., p. 49. Quoted from Charles Francis Adams, ed., <u>The</u> <u>Works</u> <u>of</u> <u>John</u> <u>Adams</u>, <u>Second</u> <u>President</u> <u>of</u> <u>the</u> <u>United</u> <u>States</u>, <u>Vol</u>. II (Boston: Little Brown & Co., 1850-1856), pp.366-368.

10. Commager and Morris, <u>op</u>.<u>cit</u>., pp. 1282-1285.

11. Maurice R. Davie, "Our Vanishing Minorities," <u>One</u> <u>America</u>, <u>The</u> <u>History</u>, <u>Contributions</u>, <u>and</u> <u>Present</u> <u>Problems</u> <u>of</u> <u>our</u> <u>Racial</u> <u>and</u> <u>National</u> <u>Minorities</u>, Francis J. Brown and Joseph S. Rousak, eds., 3d ed. (Englewood Cliffs, N.J.: Prentice-Hall, Inc., 1952), p. 549.

12. <u>Ibid</u>., p. 548.

13. Oliver Optic, <u>Little</u> <u>by</u> <u>Little</u> or <u>The</u> <u>Cruise</u> <u>of</u> <u>the</u>

61

Flyaway (Chicago: W. B. Conkey Co., nd), pp. 232-233.

14. For example, see Michael Harrington, _The Other America_ (New York: The Macmillan Co., 1962).

15. R. L. Duffus, "Getting at the Truth about an Average American Town," a review of Lynd and Lynd, _Middletown_, in the _New York Times_, January 20,1929. Reprinted in Garry Wills, ed. _Values Americans Live By_ (New York: Arno Press, 1974), p. 58.

16. Brown and Rousak, _op.cit._, _passim_.

17. Peter Steinfels, _The Neoconservatives_ (New York: Simon and Schuster, 1979), p. 35.

18. _Ibid_.

19. Andrew M. Greeley, _That Most Distrustful Nation, The Taming of the American Irish_ (Chicago: Quadrangle Books, 1972), p. xxvi.

20. Michael Novak, _The Rise of the Unmeltable Ethnics_ (New York: The Macmillan Co., 1971), pp. xxi-xxii.

21. That the child is receiving value education in a democracy is particularly important in that different political systems use different methods and content in order to transmit those values which are consistent with their political and social system. For value and character education in the Soviet Union and for a comparison of this educational system with the United States, U. Bronfenbrenner, "Soviet Methods of Character Education," _American Psychologist_, vol. 17 (1962), pp. 550-564. Also, U. Bronfenbrenner, _The Two Worlds of Childhood_ (New York: Russell Sage Foundation, 1970).

22. William K. Frankena, "Educational Values and Goals: Some Dispositions to be Fostered, "_The Monist_", vol. 52 (1968), p. 4.

23. Paul H. Hirst, _Moral Education in a Secular Society_ (London: University of London Press, Ltd., 1974), pp. 103-104.

24. Amitai Etzioni, "Can Schools Teach Kids Moral Values?", _New York University Education Quarterly_,

vol. IX (1974), pp. 5-6.

25. Ibid., p. 5.   Also, see Amitai Etzioni, "Can Schools Teach Kids Values?", Today's Education, vol. 66 (1977), pp. 29-36.

26. John Rawls, A Theory of Justice (Cambridge, Mass.: Harvard University Press, 1971), p. 490.

27. Ibid., p. 471.

28. Ibid., p. 440.

29. Laches, 191D.

30. Frankena op.cit., pp. 3-5.

CHAPTER IV

RULES and VALUES

My strategy in this chapter is to focus on one
salient theme underlying much of twentieth century
moral psychology, sociology, and philosophy. The
theme is: Moral behavior is rule-following and rule-
guided behavior. This chapter concentrates on the
fundamental position of rules in all social interaction for moral and value judgments and behavior. For
the present, I say nothing about who constructs rules,
how they are constructed, how they are learned, or
other similarly perplexing problems. We return to
these problems in subsequent chapters. My immediate
concern is the fundamental character of rules in
theories of moral development, behavior, and education.
Emphasis on rules has not always been a feature of
moral theories or education. Only since the Kantian
watershed has such rule orientation gradually super-
seded older moral character emphasis.[1] At present,
so few moral theorists challenge the tide of moral
rule that they are conspicuous on the intellectual
horizon.

Stressing rules as underlying social interaction
and value judgments may seem strange in a contemporary
book on values and moral education. At first glance,
it may seem that people have freed themselves from de-
pendency on rules. Expressions such as "do your own
thing," characterize the rejection of rigid, explicit
rules.

Narrow rule itemization is often found in traditional etiquette codes. An 1872 book on etiquette
describes dinner party rules:

> The gentleman who takes you into the dining
> room will sit at your right hand. Take off
> your gloves, and put them on your lap. Be-
> fore you, on your plate, will be a table
> napkin, with a dinner-roll in it; take the
> bread out and put it at the side of your
> plate. Lay the opened table napkin in
> your lap, on your gloves, and then listen
> gracefully, and with attention, to your
> companion, who will do his best to amuse
> you till the soup is handed round.

In ancient Egypt, a vizier instructs his son on the
rules of behavior, which will guarantee his success.
Among the rules, the vizier includes:

> Behavior in Changed Circumstances
> If thou be great that once wast humble, and
> rich that aforetime wast poor, in the city
> that thou knowest, be not close because of
> that which happened to thee of old. Be not
> overcareful in respect of thy wealth, which
> hath come to thee by the god's gift . . .

> Obedience to a Superior
> Bend thy back to him that is over thee, to
> thy superior in the administration; thy
> house shall abide by reason of his substance,
> and thy recompense shall come in due season.
> Evil is he who resisteth his superior, for
> he liveth only so long as he is gracious.[3]

In many contemporary social situations, rules are
still commonplace. While walking in the park, one
notices the sign, "Do not walk on the grass." In a
movie, a "no smoking" sign reminds us of expected behavior. Prospective brides still buy magazines and
books telling them the rules of conduct expected at
weddings. My interest here, however, is not primarily
with these explicit, itemized, or intransigent rules.
Rather, I am concerned with rules which organize and
characterize human social life and interaction. I am
prepared to argue that such rules also form the basis
of our unexamined values and the value system accepted
by our society. Most often, these rules are implicit,
unstated, and unconsciously followed. We take these
rules for granted. Through rule structures, we possess
a background, a commonsensical, comfortable, social
world, in which we can live and function without cognitive thought. I pass a friend and do not have to
think, "what should I do?" My familiarity with the
rules of my society's social interaction causes me to
shake hands and say, "hello" or "hi" or "how are you?"
without a thought. In a different society, perhaps, I
would embrace or bow to the person. Education and experience in a particular social context habituate the
person to which rules are valid for different social
contexts.

Moral and value education in general do not occur in a vacuum, nor does conscious, explicit school value education confront an infant or a babe in swaddling clothes. The student as well as the school already possess considerable tacit and explicit value and moral luggage. Family, friends, children's games and toys, television, and many other aspects of social and individual life contribute to value and moral rules possessed by the child entering school.

The importance of the child's early education is stressed by R. M. Hare when he states:

> A child's moral upbringing has an effect upon him which will remain largely untouched by anything that happens to him thereafter. If he has had a stable upbringing, whether on good principles or on bad ones, it will be extremely difficult for him to abandon those principles in later life. . . .[4]

In adult life as well, rules play a basic role in determining moral and value judgments and behavior. For example, even the recognition of a moral dilemma in life is not obvious or clear-cut. The making of moral judgments is not a logically neat procedure. The individual often experiences tension and conflict between societal morality and personal moral reasoning or principles, between social role constraints and freedom, and between personal desires, goals, and the general good.

This chapter begins with a number of assumptions. The meaning and justification of these assumptions is then investigated. Rules are shown to be a basic feature of social interaction and morality. Finally, it is argued that rules form a large portion of the individual's taken-for-granted world and thus, his basic values.

Assumption 1. The ability or inability to use rules, follow rules, and formulate rules depends on early education and experience with rules.

Assumption 2. The learning of social rules is not necessarily based on the explicit, conscious transmission of rules. Through interaction in a social world, the child learns the rules and concomitant modes and styles of behavior.

Assumption 3. For each individual, maturation requires knowledge, recognition, and acceptance of a taken-for-granted world.

Assumption 4. A person's morality and concern for moral rules is dependent on the quality of his taken-for-granted world. Even an individual's own formulation of moral rules necessitates a background taken-for-granted world.

The relation of social interaction to rules typifies much of twentieth-century intellectual investigations. Human life, social interaction, and behavior have been analyzed in the context of games with human beings playing different roles in different games. For example, the twentieth-century philosopher, Wittgenstein spells out a range of topics, human concerns, and behavior which can be treated as games.[5] Since Wittgenstein, English and American philosophers have been consumed by the study of language games as surely as Kawabata's Master was consumed by the Japanese game "Go." However, English and American philosophers often ignore something that Kawabata, in his magnificent work, The Master of Go,[6] never ignored. Kawabata stresses the non-verbal ceremonies and rituals in his description of the battle for the title "Master." In this book, there is little verbal dialogue; the non-verbal conveys all. Verbal behavior alone cannot convey the richness of social interaction and human behavior. Wittgenstein himself was never so naive as to limit language-games to the verbal alone. For example, when Wittgenstein includes play-acting as a language-game, he tacitly recognizes the multiplicity of non-verbal communications and movements, augmenting and enriching the verbal message.

In any social encounter, rules are consistent with the particular social situation and the expectations of each individual. A search for the complex features of early moral development and for the need of a taken-for-granted world begins with an elucidation of a few characteristics of rules in games, as analogous to rules explaining human behavior and social interaction.[7]

(i) The basic rules define the domain of possible events in the game.[8] Through the basic rules, the actual features of the situation are recognized as the game. Events are not random, confused, unconnected happenings. They take on meaning by being interrelated set(s) of plays. When an individual moves from one game domain to another, he recognizes a different set of rules as defining each different domain.

Playing bridge involves such basic rules, e.g., the dealing of cards, the number dealt, the order of bidding, the bidding strategy. In bridge, a novice may not possess the necessary finesse, experience, subtlety, or knowledge to understand or use all the rules properly; however, the basic rules, whether known by bridge player or bystander, exist and define bridge's environment. With social interaction, observable events and rules do not seem to mesh as neatly. For example, different rules seem to guide different dinner parties. The dinners Fannie experienced at Mansfield Park, in Jane Austen's book of the same name, were considerably different from the dinners with her poverty stricken family. Yet, even in such disparate interactions, the basic rules of each social game define the environment or possible events. If the dinner party rules at Mansfield Park or in Fannie's poverty stricken family were enumerated, any participant or observer would be able to observe and understand the interactions at each respective dinner.

(ii) Rules are invariant no matter what the changing states of the game may be. For example, if I play bridge in my living room or at a student center, with friends or strangers, in the afternoon or evening, it is still the game of "bridge," a game with identical rules.

Of course, in time, the rules of a game may change. However, within the single game, group of identical games, or for a given period of time, the rules of the particular game do not change. For example, the rules of baseball or football have changed over the last fifty years; the changes seem dependent on economic facts and on differences between radio and television. However, during a single baseball game, or baseball season, certain basic rules of the game do not change. If these basic rules did change, the game would be destroyed.

In baseball, the American League has a designated hitter rule which stipulates that a player bats in place of the pitcher, but does not play on the field. This fairly recent change in the rules does not interfere with the basic rules. A basic change might be a change in the number of strikes, balls or the number of bases. At present, any such change would open the question of whether the game were still baseball.

Similarly, at a dinner party, at a particular level of society, at a given time, the rules of conduct are more or less invariant. For example, in the Trollope Pallisar books, Glencora Pallisar tells her husband, Plantaganet, that Mr. Botting is not to be invited to dinner again, for he does not comport himself in accordance with Pallisar or even gentlemenly dinner party rules. Here, the rules did not change even though a new variable, Mr. Botting, from a different class of society, had entered the scene.

(iii) Rules serve as standards to define correct play. Rules or standards are not necessarily devised to be pleasurable, efficient, colorful, or to guarantee safety, well-being, and comfort. Rather, rules are standard(s) that are suitable, right, valid, correct, or just in the particular game.[9] In many societies, rituals are dangerous, unhealthy, difficult, and inefficient. However, even with negative characteristics, sets of rules as standards in any particular game possess internal coherence, regularity, and suitability for the particular practice.

Whether in games or social interaction, players make mistakes and observers are bothered when another's actions are not consistent with the rules. How can wrong, incorrect, or mistaken moves, plays, or actions be explained? If a player's move is outside the game's rules, audience reaction to the infringement of game standards can be graphed on a continuum. On one side the incorrect play, might be classified as strange and on the other side of the continuum, as socially unacceptable and deserving reprobation.

An example of a strange move might be a bridge player using his hand to build a house of cards. In addition to the player not following the correct rules, other participants and observers would be shocked or amazed at the strangeness of the action. Though amazed or uneasy, the observers of this card castle-building would not know the intentions of the builder. Perhaps, he was a budding ethnomethodologist, attempting to achieve exactly the given audience reaction.

If an action is contrary to the game's rules, it may be "senseless, i.e., it acquires the perceived properties of unpredictability. . . ."[10] Before one could label a card player's action senseless or strange, which "game" the individual was playing would have to be ascertained. Was the individual playing a different 'game," merely mistaken, forgetful, confused, emotionally disturbed, or deliberatively disruptive?

Antithetically, if an action is an infraction of a socially important or intrenched game or rule, observers and other participants probably will not merely be uneasy with the player's display or infringement of the rules. In strictly ritualistic, religious or social games, actions contrary to the rules may generate or require appropriate sanctions.

(iv) "Each different set of basic rules defines a different domain of possible game events that an otherwise identical behavioral appearance can set in correspondence to."[11] For example, if you are dealing cards, how does an observer know it is bridge, not rummy, canasta, poker, or fortune telling when the act of distributing cards is identical? The rules of the particular card game indicate the meaning of otherwise unintelligible behavior, i.e., the rule context gives meaning to behavior, events, and states of affairs. Intentions or purposes are revealed through the agent accepting and using the game rules appropriate for the particular intentions or purposes. For example, at an auction, an individual scratching his ear or head or raising his finger slightly signals a bid; whereas, at a cocktail party, such actions might call a waiter, relieve an itch, or display puzzlement at someone's comment.

(v) The set of all basic rules defines a game. This does not mean that all rules are equally important or basic. Some of the unimportant ones may drift into disuse or be changed, without the destruction of the game. At any time, a bystander or participant cannot be said to know a game unless the entire set of basic rules is known. Players are expected to know and audiences expect to perceive all rules.

(vi) How should action based on rules be described? Is it rule-following, rule-determined, or rule-guided? No simple expression or description does full justice to the ranges of constraint and freedom possible when using rules in social interaction. The three expressions "rule-determined," "rule-following," and "rule-guided" describe different ways rules govern human behavior. Some social rules require considerable conformity to rules. We can say that Behavior in these conforming situations is rule-determined behavior. In other social situations, the human being can interject personal interpretation and style in his use of rules. Here, rules guide behavior, allowing the individual considerable freedom. The difference here is similar to making pottery by using a mold and creating pottery on a potter's wheel. With a mold, the clay follows the lines and shape of the mold, each produced piece being almost identical. With a potter's wheel, there is great variation in shape or size depending on the creativity and skill of the potter.

In situations such as the military or a game of logic, there is considerable conformity between rules and actions. Even actions based on the rules of etiquette or religious rituals display considerable conformity between rules and actions. However, in other social situations and games, an agent's leeway, initiative, or creativity can be considerable. Style, intellegence, motivation, practice, personality, intentions, needs, cultural background, and many other factors may contribute to the way an agent interprets rules and interacts in particular social situations.

At times, an individual intentionally substitutes rule-determined and rule-following behavior even when behavior should merely be rule-guided. Many industrial concerns have become worried about workers who are merely "working to rule." "Working to rule" is a form of resistance, criticism, sabotage, through which the worker communicated his discontent and dissatisfaction. Richard Sennett explains this new phenomenon:

> . . . the worker simply obeys rules of work
> agreed on between management and union lead-
> ers. These rules are usually so far from
> the realities of work that obeying them

scrupulously will drastically slow down
the production process.[12]

The basic point here is that in a complex, western society a vast number of social interactions require
individuals to interpret rules and not merely intran-
sigently follow them. In fact, the blind following of
rules in situations where interpretation is required
causes confusion, annoyance, anger, etc.

Think what this range from rule-following to rule-
guided behavior, from constraint or conformity to freedom and creativity means for early childhood education!
The child not only must learn a great variety of rules;
in addition, he must understand when a rule or set of
rules should be strictly followed and when his creative
interpretation of a rule is valid. In all cases,
whether rule-determined or rule-guided, the acquisition
of style or grace is a further complication, a difficult process to understand and explain.

Some educators such as A. S. Neill, would probably argue against social interaction that is rule-
determined, i.e., where there is considerable conformity
between rules and action. At the very least, Neill
desires an expansion of rule-guided behavior with a
concomitant diminishing of rule-determind behavior.
Neill does not reject etiquette or polite interaction.
Instead, he only rejects artificial, externally mandated etiquette and social rules. Neill desires individual
freedom to create and decide upon the forms of social
interaction. The only criteria for Neill would be acceptance of the other's rights. This position regarding
rules can be characterized as a critique of society and
constraint on the individual through subtle manipulation.
Acceptance of Neill's position would also be acceptance
of a rule-guiding approach to common social interaction.

(vii) Rules cause an individual to expect certain
actions. In the vast majority of social interactions
an individual is expected to accept and use appropriate
rules. To say that an individual is required to follow
a rule or set of rules seems incorrect. Even if he
were required to follow the rules, a person may or may
not actually follow it. Bernard Mayo explains why the
term "expectations" is more suitable than "requirements":

. . . the term "expectations" conveys more
of what is wanted than does the term

'requirements'. Both expectations and
requirements are satisfied or unsatis-
fied, fulfilled or unfulfilled; but
expectations, unlike requirements are
true or false: they include beliefs
about their own satisfactions. They
also include beliefs about other people's
expectations. . . I can expect you to
expect. . ., but I cannot require you to
require. . .[14]

The term "expectations" is not limited to the agent's
expectation regarding the other's actions. Two examples clarify the meaning of expectation here, one
of a fairly simple social interaction and the other
from a teaching situation:

(a) As a person (the agent) walks down a street,
he notices an acquaintance (the other) coming toward
him. At that moment, the agent builds up certain expectations. The agent expects the other to greet him,
say "hello, how are you?" or some other appropriate
greeting. Depending on the culture and the context,
the agent might also expect the other to stop and shake
hands. Simultaneously, the agent expects that the other
possesses similar expectations and also, that the other
realizes the expectations the agent possesses.

(b) An examination is being given in a class. The
teacher expects students to complete the examination
without cheating. A student expects that the teacher
expects the test to be the student's work. Furthermore, any teacher would claim, however, that this set
of expectations is far too simplistic. For example,
the teacher also expects that while students are supposed to complete the examination without cheating,
many students might cheat given the opportunity. In
a case such as this, each participant in a social interaction does not merely possess a single expectation,
but the entire range of expectations possible. The
teacher should be able to accomplish this to a greater
extent than the student since the teacher is able to
take the student's point of view and envisage a wide
range of his expectations. The student may only be
able to imagine a limited range of expectations.

These expectations further strengthen the argument
that in most social interactions rules guide, rather
than determine, action. However, since action is only

73

expected, there can always be variety in the manner rules are carried out in practice: there can always be error in expectations.

(viii) The rules of social interaction often are not explicitly or self-consciously known or chosen.[15] The average individual is not a sociologist investigating the rules which guide his behavior. In certain situations, the presence of rules becomes apparent. For example, when traveling in a different country or when interacting with an individual using different rules, one becomes aware of differences in social rules. The strangeness or awkwardness of such situations often heightens awareness of rules underlying social interaction. In other words, when a situation is strange, awkward or embarrassing, we question what proper conduct should be. We realize and appreciate the social rule structure, even if the rules are unknown, strange, or seemingly incorrect. Of course, in certain cases, an individual insulates himself against the possibility that his own rules may be wrong for this new strange rules orientation. He is unable to question or contemplate the adequacy or inadequacy of his own social rules. He is unable to take the other individual's point of view.

Even if social rules are brought into focus, stated, and analyzed, a list of rules does not reveal the practice as a whole. Just as with gestalts, where the set of included items or parts does not reveal the configuration or whole; so with rules of social interaction. Their statement alone would not make one proficient in the practice of the rules in relevant social interactions.

An analysis or description of the teaching of rules and their use in social interaction is complex. From earliest childhood, the individual is initiated into organization of social rules. The first problem in understanding how the school teaches values relates to this early initiation. The teacher interacts according to a taken-for-granted world and set of rules, but is not conscious of the rules or the nature of the taken-for-granted world. Only when the teacher is unable to relate to students, fails to teach basic skills, and is faced with discipline problems, or is there the possibility of recognizing dissonance between the rules the teacher accepts and the rules students accept.

74

The method of teaching rules is a perplexing one, whether method refers to formal or informal teaching. No single method seems sufficient or appropriate for all rules. Rather, the nature or complexity of the rule(s) and psychological considerations such as developmental or understanding level, motivation and differential perceptions, guide decisions as to which method is most adequate or advantageous. In addition, because teaching methods involve social interaction, rules are often culturally determined.

Unquestionably, these comments regarding rules and games could be extended considerably. Rules and social games could be classified in different ways. Following Goffman, rules could be symmetrical and asymmetrical.[16] According to Edward Hall rules and games could possess high or low context. Further, one might distinguish between principles and rules,[17] between rules of thumb and moral rules, between discretionary rules and arbitrary rules, between advisory rules and house rules. Lastly, one might study the differences between game rules and social rules.

The remainder of this chapter consists of a number of points about the function of this rule orientation for moral and social interaction:

(i) Rules form the basis of the individual's taken-for-granted world. This does not refer to random, unorganized, fragmented rules, but to organized, coherent sets of rules, analogous to the rules of games. The world-taken-for-granted has two components, an objective world and a subjective, biographically-determined world. The objective world is the world human beings in a society have in common; that is, the physical, logical, scientific world of commonly-held values and religious beliefs. The subjective, biographical world is based on an individual's unique personal life history, --family relationships, experiences, and education. Together, these two worlds form the taken-for-granted-world.[18] Without such a world we would not be human. Without this coherent world, all would be chaos, and for an adult, such a chaotic, unorganized world would be the world of the insane.

The taken-for-granted world not only provides a comfortable, recognizable home, but affords many luxuries. The avoidance of trivial, routine matters affords the time and context for consideration of the novel and creative, the extraordinary and new. It provides the spectacles through which we see, often determining what we see and how we see. Even the problems perceived and the conflicts nagging at us are governed by the taken-for-granted world. Whether we can be educated, the character of our education, our plans, dreams and expectations--all are influenced by this taken-for-granted world. In the words of John Rawls, "each person finds himself placed at birth in some particular position in some particular society, and the nature of this position materially affects his life prospects."[19]

Is a taken-for-granted world with all its security, constraints, and limitations merely behaviorism under a different guise? The orientation here is quite distinct from behaviorism. This orientation can best be illustrated by picturing the taken-for-granted world as a continuum, a one dimensional grid, with total anarchy--the absence of any taken-for-granted world on one side and at the other extreme, the individual entirely engulfed or absorbed by such a world. Absorption would be as suffocating as anarchy. What if the individual wholly relies on a routine, never expecting or accepting change or conflict? Can such an individual survive? Maybe! But survival would be limited to the institutional life of the severely emotionally disturbed. The continuum model allows for the positing of two opposing extremes existing in dynamic tension and dialectical interplay. Only with an intermingling between the given and the unknown, the routine and unusual, the habitual and unexpected can human life continue and progress.

(ii) One of the formidable, critical tasks of childhood education is the establishment of this taken-for-granted world. The quality of later moral development and behavior is dependent on this early formative education. These claims do not spell out the content of the taken-for-granted world the child should possess. Obviously, the worlds of the eskimo or bushman, the medieval knight or classical Athenian are quite different from the technological world of the twentieth century urban child. This idea of multiple realities is valid for different children in the same society because of different biographical histories, derived from different family situations, socio-economic or

ethnic backgrounds, and different religious belief
systems. Thus, the idea of a single, valid content
for sets of rules or a general taken-for-granted world
would seem inconceivable. The idea of pluralistic
taken-for-granted worlds with their pluralistic values
presently is accepted in many societies. Too often,
however, this pluralism is not merely derived from
various sub-groups in society. Individual families
often display considerable variation from any general
taken-for-granted world. Can any society survive without some common expectancies, values, manners, moral
rules? Conflicts stemming from this question have
taken on frightening proportions. Both education and
society need to discover some unified vision that will
bind disparate worlds.

Still, one might ask: Is our search for a taken-
for-granted world suitable for moral development short
lived? Can any formal or material characteristics of
this world be enunciated? On the formal level, characteristics seem to reveal themselves more readily than
on the material level. Each of the following formal
characteristics is expanded to consider its implications or meaning for childhood education and moral development and behavior:

(a) A taken-for-granted world is based on rules and
rule orientation, e.g., rules underlying social interaction, belief, and attitudinal systems. This suggests
that actual life and moral life cannot be based on a
confused stream of unrelated happenings. The world one
lives in and relates to must be organized according to
tacit, implicit, and explicit rules. By far, the lar-
gest category of rules is that of tacit or implicit
rules.

How a child is educated to possess such a taken-
for-granted world is a puzzling question, because human
beings seem to possess such a world merely by living,
without the possession being the outcome of deliberate,
conscious training. The emphasis here is especially
crucial to the assumptions regarding potentiality for
moral development and education. The present breakdown
of the rules of the taken-for-granted world seems to
endanger the fabric of moral development and behavior.

Infants easily become accustomed to routine, re-
petition, and orderliness. If Piaget's experimental
studies with his own children illustrate anything, it

is the construction of a logical taken-for-granted world. A chaotic, inconsistent environment does not aid the child's maturing cognitive abilities. The presentation of a structured, consistent, coherent, and friendly environment does provide such potentialities.

What happens to the infant who never builds up any consistent expectations, who never knows whether he will be fondled or ignored, whether he will be played with or slapped, whether crying signals something or nothing? With different rules apparently governing identical situations and interactions, there is no possibility of building up a taken-for-granted world. Gregory Bateson asserts that schizophrenia is one species behavior derived from "some sort of tangle in the rules for making transformations (of double-binds) and about the acquisition or cultivation of such tangles (double-binds)."[20] Double-bind itself refers to the reception of two inconsistent, equally valid messages from the identical environment. From this idea, one can imagine the type of environment which does not allow for a hospitable, trustworthy, consistent, rational taken-for-granted world.

(b) The constraints of consistency apply to the rules structuring the taken-for-granted world. That is, the same rule applies to the same or similar situations, states of affairs, and cases. This, of course, does not negate the idea of the growth of an individual's taken-for-granted world. With growth or maturation, the rules may have to be restructured, but the restructuring is akin to the reorganization of a gestalt with greater complexity and increased elements.

What would not contribute to such development of a taken-for-granted world would be different rules being used for identical situations.

(c) The taken-for-granted world needs to be coherent, thus forming an overall, holistic, integrated world vision. This does not suggest that any single individual cannot possess many roles following many rules. However, all roles and their respective rules exist within an integrated world. Thus, one can imagine the difficulties concomitant with two extremes, either the non-existence of alternative roles for the child to experiment with or the existence of too great a range of roles at too early an age.

As a child matures he needs to imagine himself in a variety of roles in his taken-for-granted world. The environment must also provide the potentiality for new actual roles by which the child can view his self and understand the way others see him. This role diversification allows the child to acclimate himself to the complexities and realities of contemporary life without confusion or the elimination of sympathy and feeling from interpersonal relationships.

(d) Sets of rules underlying the taken-for-granted world must be actualized in practical life. This point is especially cogent in contemporary, technological society. Often individuals make moral judgments and have good intentions, but their will is paralyzed. The individual's will is not strong enough to manifest the judgment in moral behavior. Cases of weakness of will, lack of self-discipline, or moral courage multiply. From earliest childhood a person should realize that life is not a passive show; life is to be lived not merely discussed. Rules guiding behavior refer to actions and interactions, not analysis. Life, then, should not deteriorate into an intellectually sophisticated set of verbal minuets. The withdrawal from a meaningful active and creatively active life can be illustrated in the following way: Instead of playing games, such as Piaget's marble games which precede the use of moral rules, children passively watch games on television. Instead of playing with toys with which he must be activly and creatively involved, the passive child watches and is entertained by mechanical toys.

Will is strengthened through the discipline of following rules, and through the comprehension that action is the natural companion of thought. Piaget and others have stressed learning and the development of cognitive powers through doing.

(e) The taken-for-granted world is not a learning of concept after concept, rule after rule, fact after fact. The world presents itself to the child as a whole. Just as the rose bud gradually unfolds to reveal layers of petals, the child's world gradually unfolds to reveal greater complexity of rules and interrelationships.

79

A final word in this section refers to the content or material conditions of the taken-for-granted world. While there is not time to spell out the content of any single taken-for-granted world, the following point can be noted: A child living in the latter third of the twentieth century in a technological society does require a particular content for his taken-for-granted world. It seems reckless to claim that the poor have their own reality and values and can be happy, though poor. It would be short-sighted to say that a middle class child's world and home, which is bereft of parents and interaction, is suitable because of its material goods. The question of the content of this taken-for-granted world has not really been addressed. Though some researchers such as Selma Fraiberg, Kenneth Kenniston, and Jerome Kagan, are studying the problems of early childhood education and the disastrous effects of inadequate care and mothering during the first eighteen months of life, they are primarily concerned with the formal requirements of the child's world. While this research is important, some common values and rules within pluralism need to be discovered for the proper development of moral education.

1. Actually, there have been continuing experiments with and arguments for character education. For example, during the 1930s the Hartshorne and Mays studies were designed to demonstrate consistency of certain character traits and their manifestation in behavior. Much to Hartshorne and Mays's amazement, their studies proved the opposite-- that certain character traits were not consistently possessed and manifested in different situations. Thus, a person who was honest in one situation might be dishonest in another. More recently, there have been arguments in favor of reinstating character education. For this view, see Edward A. Wynne, "The Declining Character of American Youth," American Educator, vol. 3 (1979), pp. 29-36.

2. --"Etiquette: Dinner Party, 1872," Rules and Meanings, Mary Douglas, ed. (Harmondsworth: Penguin, 1973), p. 217.

3. "The Instruction of Ptah-Hotep," T. Eric Peet, trans., A Comparative Study of the Literature of Egypt, Palestine, and Mesopotamia (London: The Schweich Lectures of the British Academy, 1929), pp. 101-103.

4. R. M. Hare, The Language of Morals (New York: Oxford, Galaxy, 1964), p. 74, 4.7.

5. Wittgenstein, Philosophical Investigations, #7, #23.

6. Yasunari Kawabata, The Master of Go, trans. Edward G. Seidensticker (New York: Alfred A. Knopf, 1972).

7. An analysis of rules as a basis of games and social interaction can be found in Harold Garfinkel, "A Conception of, and Experiment with 'Trust' as a Condition of Stable Concerned Actions," Motivation and Social Interaction: Cognitive Determinants, O. J. Harvey, ed. (New York: Ronald Press, 1963), pp. 187-238. For analysis of the Garfinkel theory see Paul Filmer, "On Harold Garfinkel's Ethnomethodology," New Directions in Sociological Theory, P. Filmer,

M. Phillipson, D. Silverman, and D. Walsh, eds.
(Cambridge, Mass.: MIT Press, 1973 1972), pp.
203-234. For a study of different soliological
uses of rules, see Aaron V. Cicourel, Method and
Measurement in Sociology (New York: Free Press,
1964), esp. Ch. IX.

8. Garfinkel, op.cit., p. 194.

9. Erving Goffman, Interaction Ritual (Garden City,
Anchor, 1967), p. 48.

10. Garfinkel, op.cit., p. 196.

11. Ibid., p. 195.

12. Richard Sennett, "The Boss's New Clothes," The
New York Review of Books, vol. XXVI, (February
22, 1979), p. 42.

13. A. S. Neill, Summerhill (New York: Hart Publishing Co., 1960).

14. Bernard Mayo, "The Moral Agent," The Human
Agent (New York: St. Martin's Press, 1968), p. 58.

15. Goffman, op.cit., p. 49.

16. Ibid., pp. 52-53.

17. For example, see Ronald Dworkin, Taking Rights
Seriously (Cambridge, Mass.: Harvard University
Press, 1977), pp. 22-28, 71-80.

18. Alfred Schutz, "Choosing Among Projects of
Action," Philosophy and Phenomological Research,
vol. XII (1951), pp. 163-165.

19. John Rawls, A Theory of Justice (Cambridge, Mass.:
Harvard University Press, 1971), pp. 7, 13.

20. Gregory Bateson, Steps To An Ecology of Mind
(New York: Ballantine, 1972), pp. 271-278.

CHAPTER V

THE ROLE of the OTHER PERSON in VALUE FORMATION:

INTERPERSONAL RELATIONSHIPS, IDENTIFICATION AND

ALTRUISM.

1. Imitation and Identification.

In a familiar scene, three children are playing together. One girl says, "Let's play house. I'm the mother; you're the father; and you're the baby." The child who is told to play "baby" may argue about his part, but except for this initial argument, the children play their roles rather well. The "father" comes home from work with his briefcase, tells his "wife" and "child" how exhausted he is, and falls into the nearest chair. The "wife" works in her play kitchen, concocting some exotic meal, and serves it at an appropriately-set table. Occasionally, she reprimands her child, each time her voice becoming a little louder than the previous scolding. Finally, she says, "For once, can't you listen to me?!" With much accuracy, the children are able to imitate their parents' behavior. The word "imitation" is used here since there are too many unknown factors to label the behavior "identification." With imitation, the individual copies another's behavior. Perhaps this imitation is merely role experimentation to see how different roles feel or suit the individual. Children pretend they are baseball players and policemen, mothers and fathers, doctors and nurses. Toys and other objects are an integral part of this role experimentation and fantasy play. With her rocket equipment and astronaut costume, the child goes to the moon or maybe to a different planetary system. With dolls as willing "babies" a child plays at being mother or father. While an actual mother drives the family car, a child is the second driver sitting in his special chair, steering with his wheel. In group work, a student-group leader imitates the teacher's mannerisms and methods to see how this role feels. Though some psychologists have criticized distinctions made between imitation and identification and have claimed that the use of two terms does little to clarify the psychological process, both words "imitation" and "identification" are still in commonplace usage and scholarly vocabulary. The term "identification" is the most important one for us in that it refers to lasting, internalized value changes. Therefore, the psychological use of identification is stressed in this section, with imitation referring only to superficial role experimentation.

Unquestionably, parents play a very important role in the education of their children. Just how do parents influence children; and what is the mechanism by which children internalize the values and behavior of parents? Any study of identification with parents must lead back to Freud, the first thinker to use the concept "identification" self-consciously in his theory. Even though many current psychologists avoid the remainder of Freud's theory or conceptual scheme, they eagerly embrace this concept of "identification." However, Freud's uses of the term "identification" do not fully contribute to an understanding of a clear-cut, single process or product. At different times in the development of his psychoanalytic theory, Freud used identification in different ways. For example in Totem and Taboo, Freud states:

> One day the expelled brothers joined forces, slew and ate the father, and thus put an end to the father horde . . . Of course, these cannibalistic savages ate their victims. This violent primal father had surely been the envied and feared model for each of the brothers. Now they accomplished their identification with him by devouring him and each acquired a part of his strength.[1]

In a similar vein, Freud refers to a phase of infantile sexuality:

> One of the first . . . pregenital sexual organizations is the oral, or if you will, the cannibalistic. Here the sexual activity is not yet separated from the taking of nourishment and the contrasts within it are not yet differentiated. The object of the one activity is also that of the other; the sexual aim then consists in the incorporation of the object into one's own body, the prototype of identification, which later plays such an important psychic role.[2]

84

In each quoted passage, the individual desires to incor-
porate the characteristics and values of the parent or
adult. Symbolically, the cannibalism of the brothers
represents such incorporation. The oral sexuality of
infant nourishment is seen as the prototype of later
identification.

Recent theories of identification selectively re-
interpret and apply the Freudian concept that appears
in the above passages. For example, identification
through envy is fundamental to the Mussen and Distler,
Kagan, and Whiting theories of identification. Mussen
and Distler assume that parental control, command, and
dispersal of resources account for a child's envy, of
and identification with, parents.[3] Whiting, on the
other hand, points to parents' consumption of goods or
resources as accounting for identification.[4] For Kagan,
envy is caused by parents' "positive and desirable attributes." The child is envious of the adult's ability to achieve desired goals. Not only does the child
desire parental love and affection, but he desires to
develop mastery over his environment, the mastery
parents already possess.[5] With the Mussen and Distler
social power identification theory, the parent can buy
the child toys, food, clothing, can play with the child,
can take the child on outings, tell a child stories or
give parties. The parent is like a Santa Claus, with
power to dispense goods. The child's identification
with parents occurs because the child desires the power
to dispense such goods to himself and others.

With Whiting's theory, the child envies the parent's consumption, control, and possession of goods.
This envy does not imply that the child seeks to identify with the parent of the same sex. Rather, following Freud, Whiting assumes that the child associates
and identifies with the parent of the opposite sex.
The son sees his mother flattering and paying attention
to his father. This maternal flattery and attention is
a resource desired by the son; therefore, to gain the
respect of his mother the son identifies with his
father, attempting to be like his father.

For Kagan, the child's envy possesses more generalized features. The child perceives that parents can
accomplish worthwhile, desired goals. Parents can win
games, cook dinner, bake cookies, fix and drive a car,
ski and play tennis, grow flowers and vegetables, knit
and paint, go to work and parties. The child desires

to possess the characteristics, attributes, and goals of the individual he envies. Thus, he identifies with this person.

Identification theory does not suggest that the child becomes an exact replica of his parents, accepting all of the parents' values and behaving exactly as parents would behave. Identification can vary in strength, the individual identifying with different behavior and the values of different models.[6] The reasons for selective identification are many. For example, the child does not possess the cognitive or judgmental abilities to interpret all parental values and behavior correctly. Further, parents do not equally communicate all their values.

> Moral values and judgments about others may often be expressed openly (by parents), whereas certain inner states may rarely if ever be communicated in the child's presence. With the exception of an occasional apology, for example, parents typically do not express guilt and self-criticism and therefore do not give the child the necessary information for connecting these feelings with particular acts.[7]

Thus, the child does not reject or ignore a particular parental value, but may not even know of its existence.

Other psychologists stress different aspects of Freud's conceptualizations of identification, assuming identification can result from either love or fear. One theory bases identification on the child's relationship with a loved parent, while another posits identification with someone feared. Anaclitic identification refers to loss or fear of loss of a loved parent or object. On the other hand, aggressor identification refers to a hostile person's hostility. From Anna Freud's theory of aggressor identification, Bruno Bettelheim explained why some concentration camp prisoners gradually assumed the dress, manner, and cruel, sadistic tendencies of their guards.[8] Aggressor identification also explains why abused children identify with abusing parents and, as adults, become abusers of their own children.

Freud describes the mechanism of anaclitic identification:

86

> It is easy to state in a formula the dis-
> tinction between an identification with
> the father and the choice of the father
> as an object. In the first case, one's
> father is what one would like to be, and
> in the second he is what one would like
> to have . . .(I)dentification endeavours
> to mould a person's own ego after the fash-
> ion of one that has been taken as a "model."[9]

In addition, the withdrawal of love by a loved person
(mother or father) is characterized, by Freud, as a
"danger-situation," in which the child "can no longer
be certain that its needs will be satisfied, and (he)
may be exposed to the most painful feelings in tension."[10] Recent empirical evidence lends support to
the relative importance of love-withdrawal fears of
children; however, there must be careful distinctions
made between excessive, blatant love withdrawal and
minimal, normal childhood fears of love withdrawal.
Limited concern about love withdrawal seems to lead
to the development of conscience and guilt feelings.
Such concern on the child's part may even be imaginary
or based on vicarious experience such as television
programs or the behavior of friends' parents. However,
if tension, fear of love withdrawal, or actual love
withdrawal is too extreme, a different process ensues.
In studies of middle and lower class parent-child relationships, Martin Hoffman has demonstrated that:

> the child's cognitive and affective reactions
> in the discipline encounter are not conducive
> to identification, since (depending on the
> type of discipline used) the parent comes
> across as an important source of positive
> or negative utility for the child--but not
> as a locus of feeling and experience.[11]

In other words, the emotional climate of a discipline encounter is such that the child cannot picture
the parent as a person like himself and worthy of his
imitation or identification. Emotions, such as fear,
anger, or embarrassment, so cloud the child's percep-
tion of the parent and the situation that internalization of positive values does not occur. Hoffman has
found that more humanistic methods involving the use of
induction, affection, and infrequent power assertion

contribute to greater value and moral internalization.
Hoffman studied two different types of internalized
moral orientation in children, together with the parental practices leading to these orientations. Thus,
there are three orientations to consider: the conventional and humanistic orientations, and the external,
punitive discipline orientation.

a. External physical punishment and punitiveness.

Unexpectedly, physical punishment for aggressive
behavior administered to school-age boys by mothers
does not decrease the youths' aggressive activities in
school. An overwhelming number of empirical studies
substantiate the view that hostile aggressive parents
have hostile, aggressive children. Hostility is not
an innate characteristic, but develops by virtue of
the disciplinarian methods used by parents. In fact,
the parents of delinquents are highly prone to use
physical punishment and verbal attack techniques to
discipline their children.[12]

With delinquent, aggressive boys, both parents
contribute to the youth's behavior and values in the
following ways: The father is usually aggressive,
resolving his personal and social problems aggressive-
ly and disciplining his son with physical punishment.
The boy identifies with the father and imitates his
behavior. The mother permissively accepts her son's
behavior, and thus reinforces his aggression and de-
linquency.

b. Conventional Socialization.

Conventional socialization refers to an internalized value and moral structure which stresses the acceptance of societal or institutional values, regard-
less of the situation or consequences.[13] Conventionally-
oriented children are disciplined by love-withdrawal
and induction. Though induction refers to explaining
why a change in the child's behavior is desirable,
often the reasons stress how the child is harming or
injuring his parents. The child accepts parental
norms and tries to be good to avoid losing parental
love. Apparently, a conventional moral orientation
leads the child to identify with and internalize conventional norms.

c. The Humanistic Orientation.

Humanistic socialization refers to experiences
which accept institutional and societal norms, but
allow for extenuating circumstances. When human life
and humanistic concern dictate, a conventional institutional norm may be put aside in favor of the humanistic concern.[14] The parents of humanistic children
more commonly resort to induction which stresses the
matter-of-fact aspects and requirements of situations.
Though these parents handle aggression towards parent
or peer with firmness, there is "relatively little
threat."[15] In relation to temper tantrums, the humanistic parent may say, "Don't shout at me, I'm not
shouting at you. Use the same tone I'm using with
you. We'll discuss it more. If you convince me I'm
wrong, we'll do it your way. Otherwise you'll do it
mine."[16] The initial tone may involve yelling or it may
be critical, but whichever is used, it is aimed at
keeping the argument going.[17]

How can the child's identification with humanistic parents be characterized? Since the humanistic
parent's discipline is discriminating, contextually
varied, and understanding of the child's needs, the
child pictures the parents as competent and rational,
for the parent is able to mediate between the actuality of the situation and the child's needs.[18] The child
is aware of the parent's discrimination and sensitivity
to situational variation, since the parent gives
reasons for his judgment. Not only does he share his
reasons for accepting conventional norms, but he
stresses his empathic responses to humanistic values.
With this sharing, the child identifies with the humanistic moral orientation of the parent. Through parental inductive reasoning and expressed compassion and
empathy, the child integrates cognitive judgments
with empathy and rationality with compassion.[19]

At this point, one can question what other features of identification might lead to value disintegra-
tion or a lack of continued value growth. For example, maternal overprotection in many middle class
families smothers a child and creates ". . . an educational climate detrimental to all identification
with, and introjection of parental (and other) images."[20]
In this case, the mother's conduct sustains the excessively emotional identification bond far past the

age of its usefulness, thus eliminating the normal identification pattern. The point here is that parental love can be a selfless desire for the child to be nourished by the best the world can offer, or love can so suffocate the child that he forever remains in the parent's shadow, a pale image of the human being he could have been.

Do identification theories merely relate to parental influence on their own children's internalization of values, or do these theories include implications for value education in other settings, such as school or community? Jerome Kagan assumes that with increasing age, identification would have a diminishing role in value formation. The child's maturing cognitive abilities and personal goals would assume a greater role through which rational judgments determine the individual's values. Erik Erikson views the situation differently when writing about the school-age child:

> Children now . . . attach themselves to
> teachers and the parents of other children,
> and they want to watch and imitate people
> representing occupations which they can
> grasp--firemen and policemen, gardeners,
> plumbers, and garbage men.[21]

Perhaps the character or strength of identification changes with age or loses its highly emotional coloration. Unquestionably, the person with whom the school age child identifies is quite different from the object of early childhood identification; however, identification still occurs!

As the child's social horizon widens, he is confronted with many adults representing different value models. If positive value education is to be achieved, these adults have to be worth emulating. Erikson speaks of this problem in relation to teachers:

> The fact that the majority of teachers in
> our elementary schools are women must be
> considered . . . because it can lead to a
> conflict with the non-intellectual boy's
> masculine identification, as if knowledge
> were feminine, action masculine . . . The
> selection and training of teachers then
> is vital for the avoidance of the dangers

90

which can befall the individual at this
stage. The development of a sense of
inferiority, the feeling that one will
never be "any good," is a danger which
can be minimized by a teacher who knows
how to emphasize what a child <u>can</u> do . . .[22]

The main question here is the character and values of
the individual with whom the student--child or adoles-
cent--identifies as he matures and develops new values.
Who are the adults he admires? Who are his heroes?
Who are the peers he follows and respects?

The importance of the values presented by teachers
is again stressed in the following:

Values are taught by all teachers. Some
teachers teach language arts, others social
studies, others math or science, but all
teachers teach values. Values are taught
whenever an adult stands before children
and acts, speaks, and reveals his convictions. Every teacher teaches something
about values by the example he sets. When
the teacher reveals the measure of his commitment to teaching by the care he takes in
preparation, he teaches or misteaches his
students about responsibility. By the amount
of time he takes from class time to complain
about other teachers or administrators in
the school district, he teaches or misteaches
the students about work. In the effort he
shows toward student work, toward correcting
students when they are wrong, he teaches them
about what they can expect from the world beyond the schoolhouse door and he teaches or
misteaches them about character, patience,
and candor. By how he talks about the government and local elected officials and the laws,
he teaches or misteaches students about
citizenship. These "values" lessons occur
in all classrooms and they are taught as well
in places where athletics, debate, honor society, and newspaper work are done.[23]

It would be undesirable and difficult to imagine
having teachers return to the overly restrictive, publicly controlled, personal life and teaching value codes

91

of the very early twentieth century. One early set of
rules limited a female teacher's dating to work with a
male as part of Sunday School teaching. Smoking and
drinking alcoholic beverages were forbidden, as were
falling in love and marriage for female teachers.
Though presently such constraints and codified rules
are shunned, teachers themselves must be responsible
for the values they portray to students. This responsibility cannot be portrayal of an artificial role or
the limited acceptance of values for the teaching context alone. Rather, in part, the values advocated here
are those which are consistent with the ideals of good
teaching. For example, to discipline a student by ag-
gressively and verbally insulting him would not merely
be the portrayal of unacceptable values, but would be
an unsatisfactory teaching and discipline method.

However, recourse to the ideals of good teaching
as exemplifying the values accepted and personified by
the teacher is not sufficient to resolve the problem of
which values a teacher should possess. First, there is
no generally accepted list of good teaching principles
and characteristics. Though some practices are considered unacceptable or even reprehensible, agreement
about good or satisfactory teaching principles and
practices is almost nonexistent. Second, good teaching
practices do not spell out what we are looking for here,
the values and character of the teacher. There seems
to be a need for something beyond explicit practices and
methods which contribute to the values a teacher eman-
ates. Emile Durkheim believes that societal rules are
revealed through the teacher, with the transmission of
the societal value fabric dependent upon the teacher.[24]
Unquestionably, teachers should not mechanically teach
rules. Rather, through their attitude, behavior, and
belief in social order and rules, the teacher must per-
sonify rules and values. The critical importance of the
teacher as a person, is conveyed in the following passages:

> . . .nothing of arrogance, vanity, or
> pedantry must enter. It (moral education)
> is entirely brought about through the
> teacher's respect for his role or, if one
> may put it this way, for his ministry.
> This respect is transmitted through word
> and gesture from his mind to that of the
> child, where it is imprinted. Of course,

I do not mean to say that one must take
some indescribably kind of priestly tone
in dictating a duty or explaining a lesson.[25]

What enables a man to speak with (moral)
authority is the warmth of his convictions,
the faith he has not only in the abstract
truth of the ideas he expresses but, above
all, in their moral value.[26]

Certainly, this authority vested in the
teacher may accrue through the respectful
confidence he inspires in the children,
simply because he devotes himself to his
work and recognizes its significance.[27]

This same emphasis on the character and morality of
school personnel is also stressed in recent articles
and studies.

Bennett and Delattre argue that:

In all teaching and learning, the character
of teachers and administrators is a critical factor; who teachers and administrators
are and what they do make a decisive difference. Schools cannot develop character
and integrity in students unless there are
teachers with integrity and character in
the classroom with them.[28]

The most important teaching of morality is
done by living example. . . . If education
is to serve ideals of morality, teachers
and administrators must embody those ideals
in their treatment of students and each
other.[29]

In recent years, there has been great concern for the
knowledge, skills, and competencies possessed by
teachers. Even in moral education, the emphasis has
not been on the character and morality of teachers, but
on the use of teacher-proof curriculum material which
would motivate value clarification and moral development. With the teacher characterized as facilitator,
motivator, discussion leader, questioner, or guide, his
role has been minimized and has become of secondary importance. The student and his relationship to an artificial moral or value dilemma and to peers' opinions

93

about dilemma resolution has been the primary thrust of most value and moral education. The emphasis and argument here is quite different. School personnel--teachers, administrators, and staff--are the major representatives of the adult world known by students. Teachers' roles and interactions with students are particularly sensitive and revealing. Often the teacher is the one adult, outside of parents with whom children have a sustained, involved, and personal relationship. Therefore, it is natural that students judge morality and ideals based on those manifested by teacher conduct.

2. Altruism and Sympathy.

Competition has had a fundamental role in American society and in the achievement of academic, scientific, business, and political success. Individualism has been uniquely connected with the American personality and ethos. Rugged individualism conjures up images of Daniel Boone or the American pioneer struggling against and conquering nature while moving westward. This is the picture of the lone individual subduing almost insurmountable odds through his own perserverance and courage, self-determination and drive.[30]

Simultaneously, however, examples from history and literature reaffirm belief in human beings' empathy and compassion for others. In Euripides' play Alcestis, Alcestis gives her life to save her callous, thoughtless husband Admetus from death.

Even though individual acts of sacrifice and compassion can be found in all societies at all times, the motivating force for voluntarism, concern for the less fortunate, and charity in the Western world can be traced to Judeo-Christian religions. From their very beginnings, Judaism and Christianity nourished the roots of self-conscious concern for the unfortunate, the poor, sick, and homeless. For the Jewish people, such concerns were a fundamental duty intrinsically pleasing to God. Biblical stories, such as the assistance given to Naomi and Ruth by Boaz, provided inspiration and models for Ancient Jews. Early Christian assistance to the poor, sick, fatherless, and homeless was continued by later religious orders. For example, the monasteries built from the 5th to 9th centures A.D. did not merely provide religious sanctuaries for the devout and ascetic. They provided organized means for caring

94

for the less fortunate.[31]

In the United States, the altruism and sympathetic concern of the average individual is demonstrated by the extensive number of volunteer service organizations contributing to the betterment of human life in general. Various institutions and organizations receive about thirty billion dollars yearly from well-meaning Americans. It would be difficult--if not impossible--to estimate the billions given in voluntary services. It is even more amazing that eighty percent of individual contributions comes from families earning under $20,000 per year.[32]

Are human beings basically individualistic, competitive, and egotistical, or are they altruistic and compassionate? Philosophic theories, psychological and sociological studies all give evidence that human beings are neither humanistic nor egotistic, but can develop and be educated to be either altruistic or egotistic, compassionate or unfeeling, friendly or aloof.

Altruism refers to moral or value choices and behavior which benefit the other and which do not necessarily benefit the agent. It is the daily concern for another without any guarantee or thought of the agent's own interest or gain. However, the agent's altruistic behavior and judgment does not suggest the elimination of profit, happiness, or pleasure for the agent. For example, a parent sacrifices to help pay for his child's college education. A stranger helps a stranded motorist fix his car. A woman cooks dinner for a sick neighbor. If each of these agents feels satisfaction or happiness, his behavior cannot necessarily be characterized as self-interested or selfish. The original judgment to help another and the initial helping behavior could have been purely altruistic. The side effects or unintended benefit to the agent would not negate his original altruism.

Martin Hoffman posits a theory of the development of altruistic motives in which he argues that the infant's empathic distress develops into the child's sympathetic distress. An infant has not developed a sense of self and cannot distinguish or recognize another. If a strange child cries, the infant also begins to cry. Obviously, the infant does not experience actual distress, though his behavior seems to indicate such distress. Why does he begin to cry after the other has started to cry? The other's distress provides cues causing the infant's automatic or conditioned empathic distress. The response is involuntary--perhaps conditioned--with the infant unable to distinguish between his own and another's discomfort. He responds to discomfort or unpleasantness and attempts to relieve his own needs. Examples of this can be seen in hospital nurseries. One infant cries out in pain or hunger and the other infants quickly begin to cry. Hoffman states:

> . . . empathic distress is basic in the early development of altruistic motivation precisely because its occurrence shows that we may involuntarily and forcefully experience others' emotional states pertinent and appropriate to our own, but on someone else's painful experience.[33]

When the child can distinguish between himself and another, his interpersonal reactions and motivation enter a new phase. Instead of the earlier desire to rid himself of distress, the child now has the prosocial motive, "How do I relieve the other of his distress?" Sympathetic distress develops in the following sequence: (i) person permanence; (ii) genuine role taking; (iii) a mature sense of one's own and other's unique histories and identities.[34]

At the end of his discussion on sympathetic distress and the formation of altruistic motives, Hoffman presents the following four hypotheses indicating the implications that the posited theory and concomitant research findings might have for socialization:

> a. Sensitivity to the needs and feelings of others may be fostered by allowing the child to have the normal run of distress experiences, rather than shielding him from them, so as to provide a broad base for empathic and sympathetic distress in the early years.[35]

All children cannot and need not experience identical distressing experiences; rather, each child must know what it means for a human being to be distressed. This only occurs if the child experiences distress. Though parents desire to protect their offspring, such protection cannot be extended to all aspects of human life. Children need to be disappointed and experience pain, fear, and all the other emotions which make us uniquely human. A parent need not consciously plan for the child to have such experiences. It is enough for the child to be human and for the parent not to be overly protective for the child to have such experiences.[36]

    b. Providing the child with opportunities for role taking and for giving help and responsible care to others--these with corrective feed-back when he is unable to interpret available cues--should foster both sympathetic distress and awareness of the other's perspective, as well as the integration of the two.[37]

Studies have indicated that children who have pets, dogs or cats, develop the characteristics of compassion and sympathy at a younger age. This would seem consistent with Hoffman's hypothesis that children should be given the opportunities to help others and be responsible for caring for others. Without any verbal language, the child learns the pet's needs and learns that emotions and distress can be communicated nonverbally.

    c. Encouraging the child to imagine himself in the other's place, and pointing out the similarities as well as differences between him and others, may also make a significant contribution to the development of altruism.[38]

Role playing has become an integral part of value exploration in many classroom situations. As with any other method, a teacher or adult must use discretion when choosing which problems are appropriate for the child's age and which problems are too sensitive in relation to the community's values. In addition, the particular structure of the role-playing exercise would have to be developed in greater detail by the teacher. For example, the teacher might use role-playing episodes taken from student-suggested value problems. Role-playing may also be motivated by the novels or plays being read in literature or by the historical events studied in social studies. What were the value alternatives open to various characters in novels? If the student were President, senator, general, an army private, or the member of a mob, what would he have done at times of national crisis? A teacher could construct a news conference, with the student in the role of historical figure conducting

the news conference and answering questions posed by
other students acting as reporters. In each exercise
there would be a number of educationally valid goals,
and one of these would be the student's experience of
imagining himself in the place of another, thereby
gaining greater sympathy for the values, choices, and
problems of others.

> d. . . development of altruistic motives
> is enhanced when the child is exposed for
> a long time to loved models . . . who be-
> have altruistically and communicate their
> own thoughts and feelings as well as the
> presumed inner states of the persons they
> are helping.[39]

With this hypothesis, Hoffman returns to identification
and the humanistic child rearing orientation as would
apply to the teacher. This suggests that no single
value education method or exercise will be successful
unless the teacher himself is a model of humane and
altruistic values.

3. Value Development Through Dialogue.

In a study of the radical youth of the 1960s, Kenneth Keniston claimed that they sought I-Thou relationships, instead of the I-It relationships which characterized so much of Western technological, interpersonal
life. Pope John sought dialogue through an Ecumenical
Council. One of his main sources for the spirit and
meaning of dialogue derived from Martin Buber's concept
of I-Thou relationships. Carl Rogers acknowledges that
the basic tenets of his humanistic psychology arose from
Buber's dialogical philosophy.

The two relationships, I-It and I-Thou, possess
considerable importance for any study of value education and development. Instead of merely looking at the
moral domain and considering relationships between human
beings, Buber's I-It and I-Thou relationships encompass
all relationships any human being could have, whether
with a friend or stranger, tree or sunset, colleague or
spouse, painting or musical composition. All life is
meeting. All of life is relationship. I breathe, and
in breathing I relate to the air surrounding me. I
walk, and in walking I relate to the ground, the solid
earth beneath my feet. I feel the hardness of its

frozen surface; I sink into its muddied, rain-drenched mass. In all of this, I barely notice It as another. It is merely a discomfort, a condition of the path I must take to go from car to house, from parking lot to store, from bus to work. So much of life takes on this mesmerized characteristic; it is nothing more than an I-It relationship.

So much of life is viewed from a narrow perspective, from the perspective of some role and some specialized ability. A teacher analyzes a student. Is the student an overachiever or an underachiever? What are his scores on various examinations? What are his hobbies? Who are his friends? What is his socio-economic level and what can be assumed with this knowledge, or for that matter, with any other information? All of this analysis is characteristic of I-It. The relationship isn't necessarily negative; it is merely the limited relationship of a narrow perspective.

A painter looks at a tree standing before him. He notes its form and shape, its color and shadows. From this narrow perspective, the relationship is still I-It. A botanist looks at the same tree, recognizing its genus and species, its age and life history; a chemist can tell its chemicals, the elements and molecular structure of both leaf and trunk, of bark and root; the lumberman can approximate the paper pulp or lumber which could be produced from the tree; the homeowner recognizes the shade the tree gives in the summer. All of this remains the narrow, limited focus of an I-It relationship. None of these relationships relates to the whole tree. The "I" of each relationship is not spoken from the depths of the individual's being. In all of these relationships, the tree remains an object; it occupies a particular space and time.

Buber goes on to recognize that another relationship can exist between the tree and the human being:

. . . If I have both will and grace. . . in considering the tree I become bound up in relation to it. The tree is now no longer It. I have been seized by the power of exclusiveness.

To effect this it is not necessary for me to give up any of the ways in which I consider the tree. There is nothing from

99

which I would have to turn my eyes away
in order to see, and no knowledge that I
would have to forget. Rather is everything, picture and movement, species and
type, law and number, indivisibly united
in this event.

Everything belonging to the tree is in
this: its form and structure, its colors
and chemical composition, its intercourse
with the elements and with the stars, are
all present in a single whole . . . I
encounter no soul or dryad of the tree,
but the tree itself.[40]

Throughout the hustle and bustle of our daily life,
the uniqueness and wholeness of the thing itself is
avoided. Instead, we are concerned with analyzing,
studying, listing, experiencing, measuring, weighing,
and quantifying. A faulty motor is taken apart and
put back together again. A physician takes X-rays,
analyzes them, and diagnoses a patient's physical discomfort. A businessman studies and evaluates a profit-
loss statement. He consults a computer and experts,
engineers and labor leaders, designers and production
people. From the information he has gathered, decisions are made. The process of decision making cannot be criticized. It is not faulty or blameworthy;
it is financially sound and foresighted; it has considered the welfare of employees and consumer. Still,
the relationship is I-It.

I-It relationships are characteristic of contemporary science and technology. Through these relationships we have created the wonders of science, medicine,
industrialized agriculture, the wonders of television,
of jet flights to the farthest planets of our solar
system. Industrialization and technology have accel-
erated our information storehouse and have produced
material goods for the many. In Sophocles' "Antigone,"
the Chorus speaks of the wonders of human beings, the
wonders which, for Buber, arose from I-It relationships:

Many the wonders but nothing walks stranger
than man. This thing crosses the sea in
winter's storm, making his path through
the roaring waves. And she, the greatest

of gods, the earth--ageless she is, and
unwearied--he wears her away as the ploughs
go up and down from year to year and his
mules turn up the soil. . . .
Language, and thought like the wind and
the feelings that make the town, he has
taught himself, and shelter against the
cold, refuge from rain. He can always
help himself. He faces no future help-
less.[41]

The life of the I-It relationship has allowed human
beings to dominate and rule over the earth, to conquer
disease and weather, quantify everything in his environment. In all this, however, something is missing.
Buber claims that in order to survive, human beings
must have I-It relationships, but to be truly human
they must also have I-Thou relationships. What are
the characteristics of the I-Thou relationship when
the relation is with another human being?

In the normal course of life's encounters, the
words spoken may be polite and correct. At lunch with
a friend conversation may be light or serious, may relate to common interests, a sport played by both parties, or be about business, children, or politics.
There is so much the "I" would like to say. There is
so much to be communicated. Does the "I" withhold himself, avoid confrontation and openness, avoid risk and
continue to chatter? The I-It relationship is safe.
The role can be played; the masks and costumes worn can
be displayed with security.

With an I-Thou relationship the entire self, the
individual's entire being, confronts the other. Categories and classifications are shattered. The self is
set free. If words are used, they are unimportant.
We might not even understand the other's language; but
we do relate to the Other as a Thou, as a unique individual. At times, words fail. How does one express
feelings at times of sadness? Can words always communicate the meaning intended? Even if words fail,
communication can still exist. For an I can communicate
with a Thou:

A being to whom I really say "Thou" is
not for me in this moment my object,
about whom I observe this and that or
whom I put to this or that use, but my

101

partner who stands over against me in his
own right and existence and yet is relat-
ed to me in his life.[42]

The clear and firm structure of the I-Thou
relationship . . . (is) familiar to everyone with a candid heart and the courage to
pledge it. . .[43]

Whether a stranger or friends, lover or enemy, student
or patient, when an I opens his self to a Thou, it can
only be with the fullness and totality of his self. A
risk must be taken. Why a risk? There is always the
possibility that the other will turn away, avoid the
relationship, laugh or scorn, analyze or grin. All of
these are painful to the human being who has opened
himself. However, even with these risks, the relationship cannot be avoided; for it is what sets the human
apart from the rest of life and contributes to the
humane life. It is from such dialogical relationships
that values develop and bloom.

In an interview discussion, Jack Mendelsohn,
minister of a Unitarian church, asked Buber what the
lone individual could do to facilitate dialogue and
improve interpersonal relationships. What can the individual accomplish in the battle against corruption
and militaristic adventurism? Buber answered:

No one can chart a day-by-day course of
action for anyone else. Life can only
be determined by each situation as it
arises. Each person has his chance.
From the time he gets up in the morning
until the time he retires at night he
meets with others. Sometimes he even
meets himself. He sees his family at
breakfast. He goes to work with others.
He meets people in the street. He at-
tends gatherings with others. Always
there are others. What he does with
each of these meetings is what counts.
The future is determined far more by
this than by ideologies and proclama-
tions.[44]

NOTES

1. Sigmund Freud, <u>Totem</u> and <u>Taboo</u>, in <u>The</u> <u>Basic</u> <u>Writings</u> <u>of</u> Sigmund <u>Freud</u>, D. A. A. Brill, trans. (New York: Modern Library, 1938), pp. 915-916.

2. Sigmund Freud, "Infantile Sexuality," <u>Three</u> <u>Contributions</u> <u>to</u> <u>the</u> <u>Theory</u> <u>of</u> <u>Sex</u>, Ibid., p. 597.

3. P. Mussen and L. Distler, "Child Rearing Antecedents of Masculine Identification in Kindergarten Boys," <u>Child</u> <u>Development</u>, vol. 31 (1960), pp.89-100.

4. J. W. M. Whiting, "Resource Mediation and Learning by Identification," I. Iscoe and H. Stevenson, eds., <u>Personality</u> <u>Development</u> <u>in</u> <u>Children</u> (Austin: University of Texas Press, 1960).

5. Jerome Kagan, "The Concept of Identification," <u>Psychological</u> <u>Review</u>, vol. 65 (1958), pp. 296-305.

6. <u>Ibid.</u>, pp. 298, 304.

7. Martin Hoffman, "Identification and Conscience Development," <u>Child</u> <u>Development</u>, vol. 42 (1971), p. 1072.

8. Bruno Bettelheim, "Individual and Mass Behavior in Extreme Situations," <u>Journal</u> <u>of</u> <u>Abnormal</u> <u>and</u> <u>Social</u> <u>Psychology</u>, vol. 38 (1943), pp. 417-452.

9. Sigmund Freud, <u>Group</u> <u>Psychology</u> <u>and</u> <u>the</u> <u>Analysis</u> <u>of</u> <u>the</u> <u>Ego</u> (London: Hogarth, 1948), pp. 62-63.

10. Sigmund Freud, <u>On</u> <u>Narcissism:</u> <u>An</u> <u>Introduction</u>, quoted in Urie Bronfenbrenner, "Freudian Theories of Identification and Their Derivatives," <u>Child</u> <u>Development</u>, vol. 31 (1960), p. 19.

11. Hoffman, <u>op.cit.</u>, p. 1078.

12. Justin Aronfreed, <u>Conduct</u> <u>and</u> <u>Conscience</u> (New York: Academic Press, 1968), p. 317-318.

13. Martin Hoffman, "Conscience, Personality and Socialization Techniques," <u>Human</u> <u>Development</u>, vol. 13 (1970), p. 91.

14. Ibid.

15. Ibid., p. 109.

16. Ibid.

17. Ibid.

18. Ibid., p. 116.

19. Ibid., p. 123.

20. Erik H. Erikson, Identity: Youth and Crisis (New York: W. W. Norton & Co., 1968), p. 122.

21. Carl Frankenstein, Psychodynamics of Externalization (Baltimore: The Williams and Wilkins Co., 1968), p. 147.

22. Erikson, op.cit., p. 124.

23. William Bennet, "A Question of Ethics," American Educator, vol. 2 (1978), p. 23.

24. Emile Durkheim, Moral Education, E. K. Wilson and H. Schnurer, trans. (New York: Free Press, 1961), p. 154.

25. Ibid., p. 155.

26. Ibid., p. 158-159.

27. Ibid., p. 159.

28. William J. Bennett and Edwin J. Delattre, "A Moral Education," American Educator, vol. 3 (1979), p. 6.

29. Ibid.

30. For the individualism of Americans and the subsequent decline of nineteenth-century individualism, see Henry Steele Commager, "Portrait of the American," Years of the Modern: An American Portrait, John W. Chase, ed. (New York: Longmans, Green & Co., 1949), pp. 28-29.

31. Gorden Mauser and Rosemary Higgins Cass, Voluntarism at the Crossroads (New York: Family Service Association of American, 1976), pp. 21-24.

32. For the role of service organizations and private social concern in American life, see John W. Gardner, "The Private Pursuit in Public Purpose," The Chronicle of Higher Education (January 8, 1979), p. 96.

33. Martin L. Hoffman, "Empathy, Role-Taking, Guilt, and Development of Altruistic Motives," Moral Development and Behavior, T. Lickona, ed. (New York: Holt, Rinehart and Winston, 1976), p. 132.

34. Ibid., pp. 132-134.

35. Ibid., p. 142.

36. Cf. Jerome Kagan, "The Psychological Requirements for Human Development," Raising Children in Modern America, N. B. Talbot, ed. (Boston: Little, Brown, & Co., 1976 1974).

37. Hoffman, op.cit., p. 142.

38. Ibid.

39. Ibid.

40. Martin Buber, I and Thou, R. G. Smith, trans., 2d ed. (New York: Charles Scribner's Sons, 1958), pp. 7-8.

41. "Antigone," E. Wycoff trans., 342 ff.

42. Martin Buber's "Response" to Helmut Kuhn, Philosophical Interrogations, S. & B. Rome, eds. (New York: Holt, Rinehart and Winston, 1964), p. 21.

43. Buber, op.cit.,"Postscript," p. 130.

44. Jack Mendolsohn, "Between Man and Man," Congress Weekly, vol. 24 (1957), p. 9.

CHAPTER VI

BEHAVIOR MODIFICATION

A zoo is troubled with a litter problem. Visitors frequently dispose of paper containers, soda cans and bottles, newspapers, and other refuse on lawns or near animal cages. There is little attempt to use trash cans no matter where they are placed or how conspicuously they are labeled. Can the visitors' behavior be modified to eliminate littering? In a high school class, a student is a discipline problem. His unruly behavior interferes with the academic progress of the rest of the students. His academic progress suffers since his major concern is disrupting the class. How can his behavior be modified? A chain smoker desires to stop smoking. He coughs incessantly and suffers from frequent bronchial congestion. Can he change his own behavior? A child is institutionalized and cannot function normally. He does not pay attention to the therapist, cannot speak or eat, and is not autonomous in any way. Can this child's behavior be modified so he can eat, dress himself and speak?

Claims have been made that behavior modification can resolve all of these diverse behavior problems. The name "behavior modification" alone does not really provide a substantial clue to this method, for all formal and value education, therapy and self-help programs seek to change, modify, strengthen, or weaken an individual's behavior. Behavior modification is one current educational method which is a relatively straightforward, direct technology to change one's own or someone else's behavior. The behavior referred to by behavior modification is not merely physical movement or action such as the wave of a hand or the kick of a leg. In addition, less obvious forms of behavior are included, such as the ability to look a person straight in the eyes. Behavior modification does not concern itself with a person's inner states, his inner feelings, emotions, desires, or intentions. If a person claims to be depressed, this is of little--or no--interest to the behavior modifier. If the person cries uncontrollably or sits alone and refuses interpersonal involvement, then the behavior manifested would be of interest to the behavior modifier.

Is behavior modification actually concerned with

rules, or with values and morality? Can the idea of
rules be accommodated by behavior modification? Does
behavior modification even relate to our primary concern, values and value education?

Behavior modification and rules.

Behavior modification is only concerned with
changing, strengthening, or weakening behavior. However, the behavior in question is not fragmented or
unorganized. Even the behaviorists are concerned with
rules, with particular behavior following or being
guided by rules. For example, a student is usually
late for class, arriving well after the lesson has
started and thereby disrupting its progress. The
teacher, administrator, and parents decide that the
student's behavior should conform to the school's rule
about prompt arrival to class. The proof of the
student following the rule would be his behavior, his
actual arrival on time.

The acceptance of values, according to a behaviorist, would depend wholly upon the individual's
actual behavior. Acceptance of a value would not
merely be some inner feeling or state. Instead, the
individual would have to demonstrate acceptance of the
value through actual behavior. For example, if an
individual claims that tardiness is unacceptable and
promptness a desirable value, that person would normally be expected to arrive on time. If the individual extolled thrift, honesty, and cleanliness, he
would be expected to have a savings account, be honest,
and clean. Individuals are expected to implement or
manifest the values they accept. Expressed in a manner
closer to behavior modification, an individual's forms
of behavior are his values. If I eat candy, ice cream,
and cake, my claims about the importance of weight control mean very little, for my behavior reveals my
actual values and the rules guiding my life. People
interrelating socially with an agent cannot see that
individual's inner states or emotions. An appraisal
of whether the agent is following one set of rules or
another is based on the agent's behavior.

Behavior modification developed out of the research and writings of the behaviorist, B. F. Skinner.
Mention of behaviorism and B. F. Skinner causes not
only rational criticism, but emotional reaction and

107

hostility. The suggestion of social and personal reform through behavior modification immediately congers
up thoughts of the behavior control of Aldous Huxley's
Brave New World and Orwell's 1984. The Huxley and
Orwell novels picture societies in which human behavior, thoughts, desires, pleasures, life style, and
even emotions are totally planned and controlled.
This same theme of behavior control is illustrated in
novels such as Zamiatin's We, and in a number of contemporary movies, such as Clockwork Orange and One Flew
Over the Cuckoo's Nest. Given the ability and reality
of science, technology, mass media, and society to
control human behavior, it is no wonder that B. F.
Skinner's behaviorism should frighten and upset so
many. Skinner claims that all human behavior is controlled by the environment surrounding the individual.
Thus, to change or modify an individual's behavior,
attention should be paid to the environment surrounding
that individual. Three factors determine and provide
the basis for modifying behavior: stimuli from the environment, the individual, and reinforcement from the
environment. How these three elements change behavior
can be seen in the following diagram:

$$S_E \quad\quad I \quad\quad R_E \quad\quad I_B$$

In the diagram, S_E represents the stimuli from the environment which causes the individual to behave in a
particular way. The individual behavior is then reinforced from the environment R_E and his reinforcement
causes the imprinting of the desired behavior. The
individual, according to this theory, is nothing more
or less than a product of his environment, its stimuli
and reinforcement.

Behavior modification is based on a cluster of
assumptions. The following are some of those assumptions which are fundamental to value education through
behavior modification:

Assumption 1. Certain forms of behavior and the
acceptance of certain rules are advantageous for the
individual and for society. Opposing this would be the
idea that certain forms of behavior do not contribute
to the individual's or society's well being, health,
and survival. Behavior and rules are advantageous when
they increase the survival potential and efficiency of
the individual and society. For example, the suicidal

or alcoholic individual possesses behavior and follows rules which diminish his ability to survive, cope with life, and of course, are not particularly <u>efficient</u> in the fulfilling of "normal" life goals.

Assumption 2. If an individual displays unsatisfactory, unacceptable, or destructive behavior, society or other individuals have a right and even the obligation to modify or change that behavior.

Assumption 3. It is more humane to modify behavior through peaceful, positive reinforcing methods than through physical forms of punishment.

Assumption 4. Of greatest importance is the actual behavior of the individual, not his unnoticed feelings or emotions. Feelings and emotions are important or considered only when or if they are manifested through various forms of behavior.

Are assumptions 2 and 3 acceptable? Does someone, whether individual or institution, have the right to change another's behavior? Under all circumstances or merely in certain limited situations should behavior be modified? Who is to be the controller or the behavior modifier? Skinner argues that our behavior is continually affected and modified by many forces--by parents, friends, relatives, television, teachers, employers, physicians, political and religious leaders, and advertisement and non-fiction books. The structure of the environment in general, whether social or physical, contributes to or changes our behavior. However, these attempts to modify behavior are not systematic and most often are not particularly well designed or scientific. At times, they are ineffective and even counter-productive. Different groups and individuals consciously aim at different behavior modification goals for the same individual. Saving banks want us to save, whereas department stores motivate us to buy; food advertisements entice us to eat, whereas physicians order a diet; different political candidates bombard us with promises to obtain our vote; a parent lectures, screams at, pleads with, or cajoles a child in an attempt to have a room cleaned. With all these varied and often inconsistent attempts to modify behavior, the behaviorist asserts that many forces, groups, institutions, and individuals are already attempting to modify behavior. However, these attempts

are not systematic or clearly defined. Behaviorism
aims to systematize and use the findings of science to
modify behavior.

The questions regarding who is going to use behavior modification still remains. Foremost in the minds
of those asking this question is the idea that evil,
dangerous, or authoritarian individuals could use behavior modification in ways similar to those described
in 1984 and Brave New World. Even Skinner recognizes
this as a possibility, but he also recognizes that the
individual himself can use behavior modification to
change his own behavior and to defend himself against
the unscrupulous psychological attacks by dictators
and cult leaders. For example, the chain smoker could
construct an environment which would decrease the number of cigarettes he smokes each day. The following
is an actual method of value education being advocated
by behavior modification?

A Case History: Charlie was an institutionalized
adult male who could not communicate with his fellow
patients or with staff. He could only grunt. Since
most of the patients avoided him, he did not have the
comfort, warmth, or pleasure of interpersonal relationships or friendships. The staff had considerable difficulty with Charlie. He did not want to join in with
others to do "occupational" therapy or complete even the
smallest chore. The only cherished interest he had in
life was smoking cigarettes. He sat by himself, smoking
one cigarette after another. He was lonely and alienated from life and people. Nothing interested or
pleased him.

The staff of nurses, therapists and social workers
tried different methods to persuade Charlie to social-
ize with the other patients. They cajoled Charlie,
argued with him, became annoyed and angry, and punished
him. But none of these techniques caused an appropriate
change in Charlie's behavior. Charlie had not become
any more friendly with other patients.

Charlie and Behavior Modification. At this point,
a therapist decided to use behavior modification. The
previous description of Charlie's problem and behavior
was deemed inadequate. Such ideas as Charlie being
lonely and alienated or desiring comfort and warmth
were discarded in that they did not scientifically and

110

accurately describe overt behavior. As stated earlier,
behavior modification is not concerned with the inner
states or attitudes of the individual. Only actual,
manifested behavior is relevant. In addition, the
behavior modification therapist eliminated cajoling,
argument, and punishment as ineffective methods of
changing Charlie's behavior.

The first step was to decide exactly what behavior
was desired. The statement of the goal, "give Charlie
some interests and purpose in life," was unsatisfactory.
Even to state the behavioral objective as, "to have
Charlie interact, communicate, and speak with other
patients," was unsatisfactory. Since each of these
goals is far too vague and generalized, the therapist
and staff would not know exactly what behavior Charlie
should manifest. The staff finally settled on a narrow-
er aim. Charlie should be able to speak with other
patients concerning football. Many of the patients
gathered around the television set and watched television together. Charlie would be able to communicate
with his peers and the staff if he could recognize and
label certain football plays. Notice that the therapist did not aim for complicated behavior, such as
"Monday morning quarterbacking," discussing the pros
and cons of various plays. One single fairly common
football play at a time was shown to Charlie. He was
told the name of the play, such as "kick." If Charlie
said approximately the correct word, his verbal behavior was reinforced. In this case, the reinforcing
agent was something that Charlie desired, a puff on a
cigarette. During the modification sessions, Charlie
was given puffs on cigarettes only immediately following the target behavior. In time, a puff was not given
after each accurate behavior, but after a sequence of
correct responses. As Charlie learned to identify football plays and as he received attention and praise from
staff and patients, he smoked less, for there were
other ways that Charlie was receiving positive reinforcement and satisfaction. For example, even though his
communication skills were minimal, he now was able to
be involved in social interaction and make friends.
People paid attention to him, both by speaking to him
and agreeing with his call of a football play   In this
way, Charlie had formed values such as friendship and
interpersonal contact that he had not possessed previously.

Behavior modification can be used in other situations, not merely in institutionalized settings. Before discussing the way that the average parent or teacher could use behavior modification, it is necessary to understand some of the basic vocabulary of behavior modification and to outline in skeleton form the general method advocated.

1. Reinforcement. Behavior modification assumes that any behavior is strengthened if it is followed by suitable reinforcement. In actuality, the behavior itself or the response may produce the reinforcement. For example, the behavior of chewing on a piece of candy is reinforcing in that the sweet taste strengthens the desire to repeat the behavior and thus, have another piece of candy. Anything is a reinforcing agent if it increases the probability of the desired behavior recurring or if it strengthens the particular behavior. What reinforces behavior for one individual may not be particularly suitable for someone else. Though certain objects or conditions seem to provide reinforcement for many people, the only way to ascertain whether something provides reinforcement is to observe what behavior follows a reinforcing agent. If the desired consequences are observed or if desired behavior is strengthened, then the reinforcer used was suitable for that individual.

The above implies that there is a correlation between behavior and reinforcement or between response and reinforcing agent. This correlation occurs, however, only if the reinforcement follows the behavior, i.e., if reinforcement is given after the behavior is emitted. Very often, parents tell their children that they can have lollipops, pieces of candy, or toys if the children promise to behave or be quiet. The reward, e.g., lollipop is given before the behavior. Behavior modification contends that this is inefficient. The behavior often does not follow when the reward is given prior to the behavior. The efficient and appropriate method of correlating lollipop and behavior is to give the lollipop after the child manifests the behavior.

2. What are reinforcers? Reinforcers can be classified according to two general categories, primary reinforcers and secondary reinforcers. Examples of primary reinforcers are food, warmth, and drink. They are not dependent upon any previous conditioning. Much

112

of Skinner's research with mice and pidgeons is based on the use of primary reinforcers. A pidgeon pecks at a bar; his behavior is strengthened through reinforcement, receiving a seed.

Secondary reinforcers occur through the pairing of primary reinforcers with other agents considered to possess strong conditioning power. For example, attention or money, praise or toys are examples of secondary reinforcers. In our example of the modification of Charlie's behavior, Charlie's primary reinforcer was cigarettes. By linking the therapist's attention and praise (secondary reinforcers) with cigarettes (primary reinforcers) Charlie gradually became conditioned to the secondary reinforcer. In other words, praise and attention became sufficiently reinforcing that smoking was substantially reduced.

Since reinforcement is the most basic factor in increasing, decreasing, or modifying behavior, of particular importance are the types of reinforcement.

(a) Social reinforcement: Social reinforcement refers to the reinforcement of behavior through the action of other individuals or groups. Attention, praise, recognition, feedback, and applause are examples of some of the more common social reinforcers.

A general rule concerning social reinforcers:

Give praise and attention to behaviors which facilitate learning. Tell the children what he is being praised for. Try to reinforce behaviors incompatible with those you wish to decrease.[1]

Not only does the rule stress praise and attention for the behavior the teacher or parent desires, but it also notes the importance of explicitly telling the child for which behavior he is being reinforced. Since human beings usually emit multiple forms of behavior simultaneously, for example, smiling, while sitting upright, while paying attention, etc., the adult would have to note which behavior is being praised.

Example: A teacher praises a student's correct behavior. This praise could be fairly simple, saying "good" or "right" or "yes" after a student has answered a question correctly. Even body language, such as a

teacher nodding her head in assent, could provide positive reinforcement for the correct answer.

Example: A child picks up his toys and puts them
in his toy chest. A parent commenting on what a good
job he did is using social reinforcement. A child sets
the table and then calls his parent. The parent's
praise of the child's help and attractive table setting
socially reinforces this behvior. The next time there
are toys to be picked up or a table to be set, the
child will be more likely to respond in the manner previously praised.

It should be noted when a teacher or parent uses
praise instead of scolding, not only will the child's
behavior be modified, but also the adult will be reward-
ed. For example:

> Initially, Mrs. A. generally maintained control
> through scolding and loud critical comments.
> There were frequent periods of chaos, which
> she handled by various threats.
>
> When praise was finally added to the program,
> Mrs. A. had these reactions: "I was amazed
> at the difference the procedure made in the
> atmosphere of the class and even my own person-
> al feelings. I realized that in praising the
> well-behaved children and ignoring the bad,
> I was finding myself looking for the good in
> the children."[2]

Therefore, the adult found there her change in behavior
was satisfying to her, that she found her teaching more
rewarding.

(b) Material Reinforcers. Tangible objects provide material reinforcement for desired or target behavior. Toys, candy, snacks, trinkets, and clothing
are examples of material reinforcers.

Example: A child rakes up the leaves in the garden. When he finishes his mother gives him an ice
cream soda. The ice cream soda materially reinforces
the raking and helping behavior.

(c) Privileges as Reinforcers. Target behavior
is reinforced through something the individual likes.
Included here would be rights to do things such as

watching television, playing a game, attending the movies, listening to the radio, staying up late, helping the teacher, going on an errand for the teacher.

Example. After dinner the table needs to be cleared, dishes washed and dried, and the kitchen straightened. Of course, a parent could undertake this task alone. An alternative would be for the parent to suggest that the family plays a favorite game after everyone has helped with and completed his work. The game serves as a positive reinforcement for helping with the dishes.

Example. Each morning, Billy refuses to get up to go to school no matter how his parents threaten him or argue with him. When he finally gets up, he frowns, complains, and stalls, always managing to leave home with little time to make the school bus. Since he often misses the bus, a parent must drive him to school. To change his behavior, parents offer Billy a certain number of minutes of television if he gets up when the alarm clock rings. There are additional minutes of television for arriving at the breakfast table fully dressed and on time. For making the school bus, there are additional minutes. In all, of course, this does not amount to many hours of television, but enough for Billy to watch a favorite program or set of programs. This privilege serves as a positive reinforcement of Billy's behavior.

(d) Token Reinforcers. Token reinforcers refer to tangible reinforcers which in themselves possess no value. For example, marks on a sheet of paper or plastic chips possess no value in themselves. However, these reinforcers can be turned in at some later time for other reinforcers,--for social, material, or activity reinforcers.

Example. A teacher is working with a small group of students. The positive reinforcement for target behavior is a token. In this case, target behavior can include paying attention, sitting up straight, replying correctly to teacher's question. At a later time, tokens can be redeemed for other positive reinforcers depending upon the desires of the individual child. For example, a certain number of tokens might be redeemed for a candy bar, for recess, for painting time, or even for an inexpensive trinket. Of importance here

is the child's ability to redeem tokens for a variety
of desired objects or privileges. If tokens could only
be redeemed for ice cream and the child had just three
plates of ice cream, the tokens for additional ice
cream would not provide successful reinforcement.

    Example. A parent might construct a very attract-
ive poster to be placed in the kitchen or some other
appropriate place. The poster would be divided into
days of the week. Each day, the child could receive a
sticker or star to reinforce certain behavior. At the
end of the week, the token reinforcers could be ex-
changed for privileges or material reinforcers. For
example, with a certain number of stars, a young child
would be able to choose a given part of the supermarket
budget or would be able to choose a family activity
over the weekend.

    Example. Token reinforcers are in common use in
society in general. In many stores trading stamps are
given. These can be saved and then redeemed for various
objects. Therefore, the behavior of shopping in certain
stores is reinforced with token reinforcers, the tokens
redeemable for material reinforcers at a later time.

    How frequent should reinforcers be given? How
should reinforcers be scheduled?

    (1) Continuous reinforcement refers to reinforce-
ment every single time the individual emits the desired
behavior. At the outset of modifying, changing, or
strengthening behavior, continuous reinforcement is
best. Quickly, the individual's new behavior is shaped
and reinforced.

    (2) Intermittent reinforcement refers to the re-
inforcement of only certain responses. Responses might
be reinforced every few minutes, every few responses,
or at variable intervals. This type of reinforcement
is more effective, efficient, and resists extinction
of behavior. Extinction of modified behavior refers
to the withering away, the elimination of behavior
when there is no reinforcement. For example, if someone does not practice speaking a foreign language, that
language will often be forgotten. Speaking the language with someone provides reinforcement for both
speakers since attention and speech responses by each
person provides reinforcement. Intermittent reinforcement is most effective in the maintenance of existing

behavior. In other words, oncebehavior has been modified that behavior can be maintained by intermittent
reinforcement.

Example. A speech therapist is working with Jane,
who mispronounces certain sounds and words. When the
therapist first introduced the correct pronunciation of
a new sound or word, each time Jane repeated the word
or sound, she was given an M and M candy, an example
of continuous reinforcement. However, once Jane had
repeated the word a number of times, reinforcement was
not given for each example of appropriate behavior, but
merely every three, four, or five times, thus, intermittent reinforcement.

A Description of the Steps of Behavior Modification

1. What behavior needs modification? What is the
target behavior? At times, parents or teachers may be
annoyed with a child's behavior. Through criticism,
adults often pay attention to inappropriate behavior.
For example, a teacher may spend a considerable portion
of the day criticizing student behavior instead of
positively teaching the student or class. Such comments as, "Keep quiet;" "Stop talking to your neighbor!,"
"Get back in your seat," do little to stop inappropriate
behavior, cause desired behavior, or contribute to
learning. Before any further step, the teacher or
parent must decide which behavior is unacceptable and
inappropriate. Often there is a vague feeling of annoyance, but no explicit knowledge of the exact behavior
which is unacceptable. The following forms of behavior, for example, might be considered inimicable with
learning, especially when a child manifests quite a number of these forms:

a) Gross Motor Behaviors: Getting out of seat; standing
up; running; hopping; skip-
ping; walking around; rock-
ing in chair; . . . moving
chair to neighbor.

b) Disruptive noise   Tapping pencil or other ob-
   with Objects: jects; clapping; tapping
feet; rattling or tearing
paper. . .

c) Disturbing Others   Grabbing objects or work;
   Directly and   knocking neighbor's book off

117

desk; destroying another's
property; hitting; kicking;
shoving; pinching; slapping;
striking with object; throwing object at another person;
. . . biting, pulling hair.[3]

Example.

At the beginning of the year, Stan's behavior
was characterized by the teacher as "wild".
She reported that, "Stan would push and hit
and grab at objects and at children. He had
no respect for authority and apparently
didn't even hear directions. He knew how
to swear profusely, and I would have to check
his pockets so I would know he wasn't taking
home school equipment. He would wander around
the room and it was difficult to get him to
engage in constructive work. He would frequently destroy any work he did rather than
take it home."[4]

At this point, the teacher or parent must ask:
What new behavior is to be acquired? What behavior
is to be increased or decreased, strengthened or weak-
ened? There must be a precise statement of this target behavior. A general, vague, or imprecise description of the behavior is not useful and most often, is
not achievable.

Example. To say that a child should be neater or
more helpful is too imprecise. Does neatness refer to
clothing, school work, or his general appearance?
Does helpfulness refer to school, home, garden work,
or kitchen responsibilities? If the target behavior
for a child is to put his toys away in a toy chest before going to bed, this must be stated or clearly and
explicitly recognized by parents.

2. Shaping: Complicated and difficult target behavior should be divided into less complicated steps.
A series of successive approximations or intermediate
behaviors should be specified. The initial and intermediate responses acceptable prior to the terminal,
target behavior should be known. Initial expected behavior should be the easiest for the individual to at-
tain. At first, the initial response is reinforced
immediately. Then, the initial response is reinforced
less frequently, with intermediate responses reinforced

118

immediately.

It may be that exceptionally complicated target behavior will include a number of steps. The complexity of target behavior is not an objective matter to be analyzed on the basis of the behavior alone. Rather, the complexity of the behavior is dependent on the individual. For example, learning to walk for a stroke patient involves numerous steps. Even after intermediate responses have been achieved, the individual may have to return to easier steps. Therefore, the seesawing between easier and more difficult steps, between the reinforcement of initial and intermediate responses is a normal process in any effort to achieve target behavior.

Shaping or successive approximation is the fundamental method of achieving successful behavior modification. Basically, it can be summarized in the following way:

(a) The target behavior desired is stated.

(b) Target behavior is divided into smaller steps, each step indicating a behavior to be performed.

(c) The steps should be organized so that there is a hierarchy from the easiest or simplest to the most difficult, complicated forms of behavior.

(d) Initial behavior or the first step should be reinforced. The shift to a higher level behavior, to the next step, cannot occur too quickly. Simultaneously, inadequate reinforcement must be avoided, for if the shift is too rapid or reinforcement is inadequate, the desired step of behavior is easily extinguished. At the same time, excessive reinforcement should not be supplied for a lower step, for if any such excess may make it difficult for the individual to move to subsequent steps on the way to the target behavior. This movement from step to step can be seen as a seesawing process, with the possibility of moving back and forth between intermediate steps.

(e) If an individual cannot or does not perform a step, it is necessary to divide this step into even easier, smaller steps, with the process delineated above continuing for each of these smaller behavioral steps.

119

(f) The methods noted in (d) and (e) are continued until the terminal behavior occurs. Terminal behavior should be quickly reinforced, with subsequent reinforcement continuing on an intermittent basis.

Example. Let's return to the example of the child who never picks up his toys and see how his behavior could be modified using the above structure.

(a) The target behavior is: Jack will put all his toys away in appropriate places. Smaller toys are to be placed in a toy chest and larger toys in a closet, some on shelves and some standing on the closet floor. The parent may even put a picture list of toys on the chest and one on the closet. The aim here is not merely to have all toys thrown into the closet, so that they all fall out when the closet door is opened.

(b) There are a number of ways this target behavior can be divided into smaller, easier steps. For example, a parent may help Jack pick up the toys. Or before Jack enters the room to pick up the toys, a parent may first pick up two-thirds of the toys, leaving one-third to be picked up by Jack. If a parent picks up some toys, a choice should be made as to which toys are difficult to manage, with the parent putting these away.

(c) The child putting away some of his toys or helping a parent put the toys away is reinforced. The reinforcement is suitable to the individual child, Jack. Thus, if parents have a similar target goal for their different children at different times, different reinforcing agents may be necessary depending on the individual child. If a parent gives a child everything he wants prior to picking up the toys, the necessary reinforcing agent will be lacking.

(d)-(e)-(f) On subsequent evenings or weeks, the child is expected to pick up more of his toys without help from parents. Only when more of the toys are put away appropriately does the child receive reinforcement. In other words, reinforcement is not given for the first step, but for the terminal behavior, having completed the entire procedure.

Behavior Modification and Community Problems: Litter.

In many American communities, on highways, and at leisure activity locations, littering is more than an expensive nuisance. Litter destroys the beauty of natural environments and the utility of man-made structures. A number of experiments demonstrate how behavior modification can contribute to litter control. Advocates of behavior modification to control litter argue that the publicity efforts of the "Keep America Beautiful" campaign have done little to reduce the cost of over twenty-eight million dollars to remove litter.[5] There is little agreement over whether additional litter cans alone reduce litter in natural environments. Though many people would deposit their own litter if cans were available, there is little evidence to support their assisting to reduce already accumulated litter.[6] In one study, recreation area visitors were induced to pick up and deposit litter by being given a small sum of money and having a chance at a larger weekly sum. Even though only a small proportion of park visitors participated in the project, the experimenters stated that "the results suggest that small monetary rewards may be a promising approach to litter control in unsupervised as well as supervised areas."[7]

Kohlenberg and Phillips conducted a similar experiment at the Woodland Park Zoo in Seattle. By using bottles of soda as reinforcement, the authors found that "reinforcement resulted in the highest rates of behavior and improvements in the aesthetic appearance of the area."[8] This and other studies suggest that behavior modification is not very effective with a large or diverse population in a fairly large area. In fairly restricted areas, however, there may be greater potential for successful litter control. For example, one can imagine such a behavior modification experiment being attempted in the playground of an apartment house. The parents in the apartment house could determine the desired behavior, the litter control methods, and the reinforcement. This suggestion of community involvement, akin to self-modification, is well within the framework of recent empirical evidence. For example, in relation to mental health policy concerning children, it has been determined that parents do not want to be passive consumers of services, but want to take an active role in problem resolution and policy-making.[9] Through community self-involvement in controlled areas such as schools, hospitals, playgrounds, supermarkets,

and businesses, individuals' behavior would become
generalized to other situations. The result would be
greater litter control through individual effort.

Criticism of Behavior Modification

As noted earlier in this chapter, behavior modification has been criticized for many reasons.

Problem 1. Can behavior modification resolve all
value problems? Can behavior modification change every
conceivable form of behavior? B. F. Skinner was asked
a similar question. Can you give a "'behavioristic
account of the high intellectual activities?'" In response, Skinner stated:

> Psychology . . . cannot answer every question
> which is asked of it. We cannot, now, give
> "a very adequate account" of intellectual
> activity.[10]

Most examples of behavior modification presented in
social service literature such as nursing or parenting
books, demonstrate the changing or strengthening of
skills. For example, a patient's behavior is modified
to enable him to walk with crutches, rather than sit
in a wheel chair. A child's behavior is modified so
that he clears the table after dinner. Behavior modification might change behavior so that someone sits
quietly through a concert or play, but it does not pur-
port to teach the individual to appreciate or enjoy
the concert or play. This might seem to be a critical
fault, undermining the value of behavior modification.

Three points can be made here: First, behavior
modification does have a role and pragmatic value in
relation to skill formation and the modification of
fairly simple behavior. Higher intellectual activities
cannot develop unless basic skills and competencies
have become habituated. For example, if a patient refuses to walk or wash, eat or dress, it is difficult
to imagine this individual fully involved with life in
higher intellectual activities. Second, some of society's and human being's most pressing value problems
relate to these basic skills and competencies. The
label "value crisis" or "value problem" is often caused
by fairly simple, annoying, painful, or embarrassing,
behavior problems. Third, the orthodox behavioristic

approach to behavior modification is no longer pervas-
ive. At present, behavior modification includes aspects which guarantee the individuality and integrity
of the individual whose behavior is to be modified.
For example, during a dialogue with a behavior modifier, an individual might discuss which aspects of his
own behavior he would like to change, decrease, or
strengthen. The obese person might seek help to control weight. The cigarette smoker might use a token
economy to eliminate smoking.

Problem 2. Who has a right to administer or use
behavior modification? This is the main problem confronting behavior modification. Discussions of the
ethical problems relating to behavior modification are
often included in books on the subject. For example:

> One of the purposes of those of us who teach
> behavior modification will be to show that
> the consequential control of behavior has
> been and is inevitable. And yet, at the same
> time, we must point out the possible abuses
> our science could be used for. We are a
> people easily tempted to quick action in
> a crisis. It must be the behavior modifi-
> cationist himself--not the opposition--
> who sounds the cautions and sets the guide-
> lines that guard against abuses of our
> science.[11]

If we merely concern ourselves with the question of who
has the right to use behavior modification, a number of
answers can be given:

(a) In certain situations, as in hospitals, the
recovery of patients requires some sort of behavior
change. The person who does not walk must walk. The
patient who does not dress himself needs to learn how
to dress himself. This is not merely for the conven-
ience of nurses or staff, but for the good of the individual himself. Instead of experiencing frustration
or humiliation at being incompetent or alternatively,
at being expected to fulfill complicated target behavior, the use of the successive approximations and positive reinforcement of behavior modification seems more
humane.

(b) Parents and adults, therapists and physicians,

123

nurses and friends use many methods to change or modify another's behavior. In the past, many of these methods have been cruel and lacking rationality. At present, many methods are ineffective, inhumane, and costly. Why shouldn't a method be used which is both humane and efficient?

(c) Anyone using behavior modification cannot merely posit some irrational terminal or target behavior without considering how it will affect the life of the individual and society. A value and moral judgment is ultimately tied to the decision that certain behavior should be modified. A nurse modifies a patient's behavior so that the patient's life becomes more meaningful, worthwhile, or humane. What is the quality of life for the individual who languishes in bed, unable to walk, dress or feed himself? A parent modifies a child's behavior by having the child help around the house so that this behavior will become generalized. Then, when the child is older, he or she will be helpful in other ways.

When it is said that the individual who is the behavior modifier must consider the value or moral implications of the target behavior, the following is suggested: In any behavior modification situation, various responses could be sought. Which response is considered most adequate is a decision the behavior modifier must make. Such a decision involves choosing among a number of alternatives. Just as a physician must choose from alternative treatments, the behavior modifier must choose, and choice must be evaluated dependent upon goals, value and moral principles, and the rights and welfare of the person whose behavior is to be modified.

(d) The individual could decide to modify his own behavior, using the same procedure indicated above. In other words, the individual himself could monitor his own behavior, decide which behavior needed strengthening, change or weakening, decide how to reinforce the desired behavior, and then implement a schedule of reinforcement of acceptable behavior.

An example of such self-administered behavior modification can be found in The Autobiography of Benjamin Franklin. After deciding to embark on a project of moral perfection, Franklin notes that, at any time,

he could not concentrate on all virtues or habits.
Therefore, he turned to a different method. The first
step of his method was to list the thirteen virtues
he desired to acquire--temperance, silence, order, resolution, frugality, industry, sincerity, justice,
moderation, cleanliness, tranquility, chastity, and
humility. He then decided to concentrate on a single
virtue at a time, starting with the first one, temperance. Franklin constructed a small book in which he
evaluated whether he had committed any fault against
the desired virtue. With temperance, he desired to
keep a "cool head" and to this end he decided: "Eat
not to dullness; drink not to elevation." During the
week given over to strengthening temperance, Franklin
marked any infractions in his book:

> . . .if in the first week I could keep my
> first line, marked T (temperance) clear of
> spots, I suppose the habit of that virtue
> so much strengthened, and its opposite
> weakened, that I might venture extending
> my attention to include the next . . .(virtue).[12]

As time passed, there were fewer and fewer infractions
against the desired new virtues. Finally, with his virtuous habits strengthened, Franklin concentrated on
another virtue. Regarding this method, Franklin states:

> . . . like him who, having a garden to weed,
> does not attempt to eradicate all the bad
> weeds at once, which would exceed his reach
> and strength, but works on one of the beds
> at a time, and having, accomplished the first,
> proceeds to a second, so I should have, I
> hoped, the encouraging pleasures of seeing
> on my pages the progress made in virtue, by
> clearing successively my lines of their
> spots, til in the end . . . I should be
> happy in viewing a clean look.[13]

NOTES

1. Charles H. Madsen, Jr., Wesley C. Becker, and Don R. Thomas, "Rules, Praise, and Ignoring: Elements of Elementary Classroom Control," Classroom Management: The Successful Use of Behavior Modification, K. D. O'Leary and S. G. O'Leary, eds. (New York: Pergamon Press, Inc., 1972), p. 125.

2. Ibid., p. 131.

3. Wesley C. Becker, Charles H. Madsen, Jr., Carole Revelle Arnold, and Don R. Thomas, "The Contingent Use of Teacher Attention and Praise in Reducing Classroom Behavior Problems," Classroom Management, K. D. O'Leary and S. G. O'Leary eds. (New York: Pergamon Press, Inc., (1972), p. 95.

4. Madsen, et. al., op.cit., p. 118.

5. R. B. Powers, J. G. Osborne, and E. G. Anderson, "Positive Reinforcement of Litter Removal in the Natural Environment," Journal of Applied Behavior Analysis, vol. 6 (1973), p. 579.

6. Ibid., p. 580.

7. Ibid., p. 579.

8. R. Kohlenberg and T. Phillips, "Reinforcement and Rate of Litter Depositing," Journal of Applied Behavior Analysis, vol. 6 (1973), p. 391.

9. Anthony M. Braziano, "Parents as Behavior Therapists," Progress in Behavior Modification, M. Hersen, R. M. Eisler, and P. M. Miller, eds., vol. 4 (New York: Academic Press, 1977), pp. 251-254.

10. T. W. Wann, ed., Behaviorism and Phenomenology (Chicago: Phoenix Books, (1964), p. 99.

11. Roger W. McIntire, "Ethical Responsibilities of Teaching Behavior Modification," Teaching Behavior Modification, S. Yen and R. W. McIntire, eds. (Kalamazoo, Mich.: Behaviordelia, Inc., 1976), p. 1.

12. Franklin, Benjamin, The Autobiography of Benjamin Franklin (Boston: Houghton MIfflin Co., 1928), p. 98.

CHAPTER VII

VALUES CLARIFICATION

Values clarification recognizes the confusing over-abundance of values facing any individual living in a contemporary technological society. The individual himself must decide which values are most important and worth pursuing. No longer are the various institutions and segments of society agreed on the values to be cherished and to guide life. In the past, identical fundamental values were shared by different societal levels and groups. The home accepted society's values and society often seemed an extension of the home. When a child left his home for school, he found the same values presented. It was not necessary to learn new values. When he left school for the greater society, the values remained consistent with those he had formed in home and school. For example, the child's attendance at New England town meetings prepared him for participation in democratic life. This consistency of values in home, school, and society is no longer apparent.

Parents and teachers often disagree about values. Different radio and television programs present different values. In fact, often within a single program, characters portray and accept different, contradictory values. News programs do not merely present facts. In addition, they expound different interpretations of the facts, different editorial positions. The President does not merely speak to the nation, with everyone accepting his programs and policies. Immediately following his speech, analysts and editors present different views of the speech. Many daily newspapers not only include letters to the editor, but even "Op-Ed" pages, featuring articles with viewpoints contrary to the newspapers' editorial policies. Other dailies include advice columns, what to buy, how to resolve personal problems, what is in style, which restaurants are worth recommending, how to raise children, and how to invest money. Friends and neighbors, politicians and religious leaders, hucksters and writers profess different values and entice the individual to align himself with their values orientations. Should the individual follow or accept the values of another person or group? Which person's or group's values are best or right for the individual? Should the individual choose his own values?

According to the advocates of values clarification, some individuals experience confusion in their lives and are unable to make value choices. These individuals may be apathetic, flighty, uncertain, or inconsistent. They may also be drifters or overconformers, irrational dissenters or excessively involved with posturing or role playing.[1]

Rath, Harmin, and Simon assume that the methods or strategies of values clarification achieve two goals. First, individuals form a clear view of their values and thus, "deal . . . with life in a consistent and purposeful way."[2] They become "positive, purposeful, enthusiastic, (and) proud."[3] Their lives possess meaning and richness, vitality and self-fulfillment.[4] Second, values clarification is concerned with socially constructive goals, with liberty, justice, freedom, and equality[5] These values will not merely be verbally acknowledged, but more importantly, will be the guides and standards for the individual's behavior and life.

What is Values Clarification?

With these goals in mind, values clarification attempts to resolve the following problem: What methods or strategies can be used to develop people with meaningful and purposeful lives who simultaneously are concerned with socially constructive values? The search is not for the values which are best for all people, but the process by which individuals make value judgments. Values clarification addresses itself primarily to the question: What is the process of valuation? The values and value problems considered are not limited to morality, but extend to all the values and individual encounters in life. Health, sex, religion, politics, fashion, art, television, work, leisure sports and activities, friendship, family interrelationships, hobbies, and school activities are only a few categories examined by values clarification.

At no time does values clarification advocate any particular or specific value. The individual himself must decide which values are worthwhile. With new experiences and changing conditions, the individual might have to question the adequacy of previously accepted values. Should the new values be accepted or rejected? Can new values be integrated with older values? Writers about values clarification do not suggest which values are right or wrong, just or unjust, acceptable or unacceptable, beautiful or ugly. Rather, the emphasis is on the process of choosing. What method or strategy can individuals use to choose their own values? Values clarification proposes seven requirements to describe the process of valuing or choosing values.[6] Basically, these seven requirements are seven steps by which an individual resolves a value dilemma or decides which values(s) he should accept. The seven requirements of values clarification are based on the method of valuation proposed by John Dewey earlier in the twentieth century.[7]

Returning to Dewey as the original motivating theory and roots of values clarification requires some further explanation. Supplementing values clarification with ideas from John Dewey's theories resolves many of the criticisms lodged against values clarification and gives greater credibility to the values clarification strategies. At times, values clarification has been criticized as being overly relativistic, as involving individualistic, narrow concerns, and even allowing only for self-interested, egotistic desires and values.[8] The values clarification strategies have been likened to pleasant games without depth and without actual education and value consequences.[9] For example, in one strategy, individuals are supposed to rank answers to a number of questions; that is, they are supposed to indicate their preferences in concrete situations. Included are the following:

a) Which would you least like to be?

_____ a rifleman firing point blank at the charging enemy
_____ a bomber on a plane dropping napalm on an enemy village
_____ a helicopter pilot directing a naval bombardment of enemy troops.

b) Which would you rather do on a Sunday morning?
_____ sleep late
_____ play with a friend
_____ watch TV.

c) Which would you be most likely to do about a person who had bad breath?
_____ directly tell him
_____ send him an anonymous note
_____ nothing.[10]

130

Since the individual must rank order the alternative
answers, there is no possibility of rejecting all the
choices and constructing a different set of values.
Even though a person's bad breath may be annoying, one
might be concerned about this person's feelings and
thus not want to cause pain or embarrassment. Yet send-
ing an anonymous note or doing nothing may be equally
cruel or uncaring. Is there a different alternative?
The values clarification question and alternatives seem
to indicate there are only three. Is this true? The
three suggestions regarding Sunday morning do not leave
room for the person who really wants to attend church.
Though the student can pass and not respond to a particular question, the very wording of the questions and
alternatives implies acceptable values. Furthermore,
one might wonder how many times a student would actually pass and refuse to answer a question.

Studies of the effect of values clarification have
not revealed outstanding, positive results. However,
for a number of reasons, this method should not be
wholly abandoned. First, the strategies of values clarification are easily understood and used by teachers
and other adults. Second, these strategies are not
unique to values clarification alone, but are exceptionally similar to those of decision making theory, critical thinking and reasoning in general. The values clarification developers have encapsulated aspects of the
basic process. However, their presentation is often
flawed in a number of ways. For example, too little
detail about and exploration of the choosing process
is furnished for the practitioner to take the strategies
past the game stage. Too much attention is given to
specific examples and too little to the method itself.
Second, no long term or proximate goals are enumerated.
Thus, often the strategies simultaneously proceed in
many directions.

By including ideas from John Dewey, the charges of
extreme relativism and individualism can be avoided.
For Dewey, an individual's unexamined desires cannot
form the basis of his value choices. The individual
alone is not supreme, but requires social life and interaction for both survival and the good life. Even
though the individual chooses many of his values, Dewey
believes that many values are determined by past experience, habits, and the requirements of social living.
Furthermore, democracy is considered the best form of

131

government since it allows for the growth and progress of both society and the individual. However, the democratic process is not a process of following unexamined desires and blind, emotional wants; democracy flourishes with intelligent, rational processes, through reflective thinking and the examination of societal values. This is as true for the individual as for the society. The combination of value clarification strategies with John Dewey's comprehensive ideas provides one valid, well-grounded, holistic way of approaching value education.

The following are the seven steps of values clarification by which values can be effectively chosen:

1. Choosing freely.
2. Choosing from among alternatives.
3. Choosing after thoughtful consideration of the consequences of each alternative.
4. Prizing and cherishing.
5. Affirming.
6. Acting upon choices.
7. Repeating.

The remainder of this chapter delineates each of these steps providing examples of their use in various settings.

1. Choosing Freely.
    The individual himself must freely choose his own values. Values cannot be the products of some explicit or implicit form of coercion. If a student chooses a value to please a teacher or earn a higher grade, the value is not freely chosen. If an employee chooses a value to gain promotion or because the employer threatens reprisal, the value is not freely chosen. If a child chooses a value to placate an aggressive, abusing parent, the value is not freely chosen. Especially for the developing student, the educational climate must be nonthreatening and noncoercive so that independent values can be chosen.

Dewey was especially critical of the fact that individuals avoid making value choices. There are so many maneuvers an individual can use to avoid making a value choice. The individual can merely drift, ignoring the value problem, postponing decisions indefinitely from day to day; an authority can be consulted or cited, whether one's parents or employer, an organization or

book; the individual could rationalize and intellectu-
alize the issue or value. By discussing the value
indefinitely, the individual may seem to be involved
with a value judgment, but really avoids making a personal judgment.

There are other reasons, however, why an individual may not be able to make a value judgment, and these
reasons may not merely be based on excuses or avoidance of the problem. The value issue may be so difficult that the individual cannot even understand the
dimensions of the actual problem. For example, if a
young child is confronted with too difficult a problem,
he may not recognize that he has a problem. Many adults,
on the other hand, when confronted with an overly difficult problem "freeze," become emotionally paralyzed,
or experience shock. In other words, if the problem is
too difficult, the individual cannot attempt to resolve
it.

Simultaneously, if a value problem is too simple,
it does not require thought or choice. The individual
relies on habit or past experience. For children especially, it is important that value problems be neither
too difficult nor too simple, but consistent with the
child's age, maturation, cognitive ability, and past
experience. In this way, the child will confront value
problems of graduated difficulty and will have continuous experience making value choices.

Example. A values clarification exercise with high
school students might involve dating practices and various value aspects of sex education. However, with first
and second graders, values clarification would involve
very different problems, such as playing fairly or attending parties. By modifying problems and strategies
dependent on the experience, age and maturity of students, the teacher can avoid value problems which are too
difficult or too simple.

Raths, Harmin, and Simon suggest a number of "clarifying responses" or questions so that students can
judge whether they are choosing freely. For example,
the teacher might ask:

    a. Where do you suppose you first got that
       idea?
    b. How long have you felt that way?
    c. Are you the only one in your crowd who feels

this way?[11]

Basically, the individual is being asked whether the values are really his and whether they were actually freely chosen.

2. Choosing among Alternatives.

Any discussion of choice or evaluation must by definition include alternatives. If there are not alternatives, there is also no choice. For human beings to live, they must breathe. There is no choice in this matter. For fish to live, they must be in water. There is no choice in this matter. However, when an individual shops in a supermarket or department store, the choices are many.

A young child may experience difficulty recognizing the many alternative values or forms of behavior possible in a given situation. The child may be emotionally attached to one alternative and thus not even notice the other alternatives. This is one reason why values clarification through classroom discussion may be so effective. Other students may suggest alternatives that the child does not see or refuses to recognize. In addition, the teacher in such a discussion would motivate students, through questioning, to discover additional alternatives.

An important aspect of this step is that the individual actually know what the alternative is. Having a value feeling or intuition about the alternative value is unacceptable. The alternative values need to be stated accurately and clearly. This is not a simple matter. For the young child, with limited cognitive maturation and experience, the statement of the value may be incomplete. Even for the adult, the intellectualization of the value alternatives is not always simple, for as the individual matures and acquires greater cognitive skills, knowledge and experience, he confronts and recognizes more difficult, complex value alternatives. This might add confusion, rather than increase his decision making and intellectual ability; however, the clear statement of the actual value alternatives brings the individual one step closer to a value decision. With the statement of alternatives, the individual recognizes and understands which values are in question; he is not merely confused, depressed, or anxious.

Example. A teacher narrates a particular value situation and asks students to list the possible alternative solutions. Since values choice means deciding upon an alternative, the teacher would also ask students to choose the one alternative they prefer.

Sample Situations.

a. You are pushing a shopping cart in a supermarket and you hear a thunderous crash of cans. As you round the corner, you see a two-year old being beaten quite severely by his mother, apparently for pulling out the bottom can of the pyramid. Ideally, what would you do?[12]

b. A group of young boys went into a neighborhood candy store every day after school. At first everything was all right, but soon they began to take things without paying for them. One day the owner caught them, and they admitted to him that they had been stealing candy for quite a while. What should . . . (the owner) do . . .?[13]

Example. The teacher shows a filmstrip or picture story of a particular value problem and asks students to list alternative solutions, then choose one alternative. This may be particularly effective with younger children or students who need visual motivation.

3. Choosing after Thoughtful Consideration of the Consequences of Each Alternative.

Of course, choices between alternatives can be made impulsively or thoughtlessly. The individual is in a hurry, annoyed at having to waste time with some activity, is concentrating on something else, or is confused. Without thinking, he accepts a particular value. In some cases this might not have much impact on his life, for example, when he buys an exotic food that no one in the family eats. However, at other times, an impulsive choice of values can have serious effect on the individual's life. A person is "fed up" with life and joins a distant commune or cult. By examining the various alternatives and their respective consequences more carefully, he might have shunned that choice. Perhaps a change of job, additional education, or merely a new hobby would have proved better choices.

The acceptance of any value has consequences for the individual in that his values determine the character and quality of his life. His values determine how he looks at himself and how others judge him, what jobs he aspires to and how healthy he is, who his friends are and how he raises his children. Therefore, the analysis of the consequences of various alternatives is actually the evaluation of what life the individual desires.

Any value choice has consequences and, for Dewey, the heart of choosing is rationally weighing these various consequences. As an individual matures and practices values clarification, the variety and respective importance of the consequences of alternatives can be judged with greater accuracy. There are four general types of consequences: short-term and distant consequences, personal and social consequences. Children easily recognize the immediate consequences and, to a limited extent, recognize personal consequences of judgments and actions, but have difficulty understanding the distant and social consequences.

Example. A child is playing with his toys. His mother suggests that he complete his homework. The child refuses, saying that he is enjoying his play. Later he will have no time for the homework since there is an interesting television program.

The Consequences. The child recognizes the immediate consequence, that he is enjoying his play. The only personal consequence the child perceives is the pleasure of playing with his toys and watching television. He does not recognize the personal implications of forming good work habits. The distant consequence, not recognized by the child, may be a failing grade for not submitting homework and failing an examination based on the homework. The social consequences might relate to the attitude of the teacher. The child might have to accept a lecture by the teacher or explain his missing homework.

These four types of consequences--personal, social, immediate, or distant-apply to all value judgments. No matter which type, consequences can also be positive (pro) or negative (con). In addition, some consequences are relatively unimportant, while others have considerable importance.

Example. The desiring of something. Jane desires a new car. Actually, this dilemma could be presented by the more general statement, A desires X, where A represents any individual desiring something and X represents the value desired. At the first stage, that of desiring a new car, Jane's relationship to the car may be purely emotional. The evaluation procedure has not started. Jane may be merely daydreaming in the same way one imagines a fairy godmother resolving all problems. In this momentary flight of fancy, as quickly as she thought of the idea, it disappeared. Of course, some individuals continue to daydream, continue to imagine that a fairy godmother will resolve all value problems. But daydreaming alone does not resolve value problems; therefore, Jane must begin a dramatic rehearsal, evaluating all the consequences of buying a new car. In Jane's dramatic rehearsal, she notes the following consequences:

Personal Consequences. Jane is pleased with her new car and enjoys driving it. In addition, she is more confident about her ability to travel from her inconveniently located home to various destinations and arrive promptly. This consequence is positive, but without additional information, there is no way to weigh the relative importance of the consequence. If Jane severely lacked confidence and had a poor self-image, this consequence might be of considerable importance; however, if there were no such problems, it might be weighted as relatively less important, when compared with other consequences.

Social Consequences. Jane's friends admire her new car and seek Jane's companionship. Jane's employer notices her prompt arrival each morning and is pleased, even though the employer does not know the cause of her new promptness. Jane's parents are pleased with Jane's willingness to help with various household errands. This set of consequences also is positive. If Jane had been on the verge of losing her job because of tardiness, this one consequence of purchasing a new car might be weighted heavily. Basically, with social consequences, the individual is ascertaining how his value choice will be evaluated by others and will affect others.

Immediate Consequences. Of course, Jane's pleasure at driving a new car is an immediate consequence. Also, Jane is not annoyed or upset about repair problems and

137

thus is calmer and more sociable. Again, these are positive consequences, even though they might not be relatively important.

Long-term Consequences. By purchasing a new car, Jane assumes her saving in gasoline consumption and her elimination of expensive repairs will offset the monthly expense of repaying the car loan. Is this really the case? Here, long-term consequences would have to be effectively evaluated to judge whether they are really positive or negative and to judge their relative weight. If Jane's expenses increased so considerably that Jane was forced to take a second job to maintain the car, the consequences might be negative and relatively important. In other words, the consequences might be so negative that Jane would not buy the car.

One of the most difficult aspects of value discrimination and judgment is the prediction of consequences. Children often do not possess a conception of time sufficient to understand or judge long-term consequences. Even adults find it difficult to predict exactly what consequences will occur in the future. However, practice at judging consequences can improve one's ability to predict realistically the effects of actions and values.

Example. A teacher constructs a set of consequence cards. Each card includes a simple statement of a situation or action. Students state all possible personal effects for any situation. In other words, if a student were the agent involved in the particular action, what would the personal consequences of the action be? After the statement of the personal consequences, the students would then examine the effects for other individuals or institutions. The following are a few situations or actions which could be included:

a. Someone dares someone else to climb a water tower.[14]
b. Someone tells her friends she can swim when she cannot.[15]
c. Someone continues his normal life though he has an infectious disease.[16]
d. An individual does not return books which he borrowed.[17]

Let's look at how (b) could be used in a class. The girl who said that she could swim, even though she could not, might experience the following consequences. Her friends might push her into the water. They might challenge her to a race and she would become embarrassed when her lie was revealed. In addition, there would be a long-term, personal consequence in that with repeated fabrication, the girl might be more likely to lie in any given situation.

When searching for the consequences for others, the class might develop the following possibilities:

a. The friends: The friends discover she has been lying and do not trust anything the girl says. In addition, the friends avoid her company, feeling she is a person they cannot trust.

b. Parents: The girl's parents find out about the incident and are quite angry. They confine the girl to the house and attempt to curb her behavior in other ways.

c. The lifeguard: When she begins to drown, the lifeguard must jump in and save her. Since he is not at his post during this time, other people's lives are in danger.

d. The newpapers: The newspapers report the incident, noting that the friends had a perfectly valid excuse for pushing the girl into the water. They had assumed she could swim. With this statement, people reading the newspapers suspect that the girl lied.

e. Teachers: Reading the newspapers, teachers are not certain whether the girl normally tells the truth or not. Though these consequences may sound rather far-fetched, they do provide students with practice through which they realize that value decisions do not merely affect the single individual at the time of action. Rather, the consequences of any action may be similar to throwing a pebble into water. There are ripples or consequences that continue through time and affect a larger area than that of the original action.

The problem of ascertaining alternative consequences becomes even more complicated when the individual is confronted by a number of alternative values or solutions to a value problem. If only one alternative can be carried out, the individual must choose the one alternative. How does he make this choice? Dewey claims that one step in this process is to examine the consequences of all the alternatives. For example, an individual has

139

accumulated money in a savings account. With his savings, a number of alternative values can be chosen: He
could a) take a vacation; b) buy presents for the entire family; c) refurnish his apartment; d) have repairs completed in his apartment or on his car; e) don-
ate part of the money to charity and use the rest to buy
season tickets to the ice hockey games. If the individual has only a limited sum available, it obviously is
not possible to do all the things he might value. How
is the choice made? One way is to list all the alternative values and then the consequences--personal, social,
immediate, long-term--for each of the alternatives. By
determining the relative importance of the respective
consequences, some alternative values can be eliminated
and with continuing eliminations and successive approximations, a final choice can be made.

At this point, someone may claim that such a process is time-consuming and tedious. Two answers can be
given to such a claim. First, if a child is taught to
evaluate simpler alternatives in this manner, then, as
an adult, the process will be fairly easy and a matter
of habit. Second, an individual would hardly be expected to calculate all values and actions in this manner,
for if he did, every moment of his life would be consumed with value calculation. However, there are times
when value decisions are so important and critical for
an individual's future life and happiness that the ex-
penditure of time and effort to assess alternative values and their consequences in practice is most worthwhile.

Additional Comments about and Examples of Alternatives
and Consequences.

A value or moral dilemma is a dilemma because there
is no one single solution. In other words, if there
were only one way of behaving or one answer, there would
be no dilemma. Perhaps, a person could explain why he
did what he did, but this would only mean referring to
the accepted rule. With most moral and value dilemmas,
there are no easy answers. Rather, there are numerous
alternative solutions with each possible alternative
opening up the possibility of different consequences.
Actually, any single alternative solution may imply
quite a number of consequences or side effects. Thus,
the individual would not merely have to note alternatives, but the consequences of each alternative.

140

Example. A group of students take an examination
from the teacher's desk. They offer to give the exam
to Carol who had no knowledge of the students' original
action. What are the various alternative actions and
consequences open to Carol?

Alternative actions

Consequences

(a) Carol accepts the examination
(a) The teacher does
not realize the examina-
tion had been taken and
Carol passes the examina-
tion. The next time she
has an opportunity to use
an examination, she does
so more easily.

(b) Carol accepts the examination. (b) The teacher realizes the examination had
been taken and constructs
a new one, unknown to the
students. Carol fails the
new examination and the
teacher believes Carol´
stole the original.
Carol's parents are called
to school and Carol is sus-
pended from school for her
part in the episode.

(c) Carol refuses to take the examination and use it.
(c) The students who took
the examination laugh at
Carol's honesty.

(d) Carol goes to the teacher to tell the teacher what
    happened.
(d) The students realize
what Carol has done, and
are angered. Carol is no
longer invited to any
student functions.

(e) Carol explains to the students in question why she
will not use the examination. She has studied very
hard, does not want to endanger her chance for a good
grade, etc. She even asks them whether they would
have taken the examination if they had studied.
(e) The students are some-
what irked, but forget
their annoyance within a
short period of time.
Carol did not receive a
perfect grade on the examination, but was not

141

bothered by her decision.
(f) Carol went home and discussed the problem with her
parents, a brother, or sister.

> (f) In the discussion, she
> was able to air many of
> the concerns and thoughts
> she had. The decision
> still was not an easy one,
> but the discussion clari-
> fied the various issues
> for her.

In the Schools Council Project in Moral Education,
the Life-line Program, there is practice in judging what
the consequences of action could be. The following are
a few of the alternative actions for which students are
to give possible consequences:
> Someone leaves cans, bottles, or bags lying
> around in the country.
> Someone runs a car engine in a closed garage.
> Someone ignores a call for help because he
> thinks that the person may be drunk or fooling
> around.
> Someone locks a child in a room.
> Someone teases a friend for being cautious
> while he is driving, (sailing, or riding).[18]

At home, a parent might ask a child about the consequences of some contemplated behavior. In a classroom, a
teacher would organize the study of consequences in a
more systematic manner. For example, the teacher might
give the students five minutes to write all the possible
consequences of an action.[19] He might list all the various people, objects, conditions, or animals involved
with the value problem and ask the students to list one
or two consequences for each.

4. Prizing and Cherishing.

Prizing and cherishing are part of the "pro" attitude an individual has towards his values. An individual
does not accept values which he is uncomfortable with,
dislikes or hates. The values accepted are cherished,
desired, cared for, wanted needed, and prized.

This does not indicate that all cherished values
involve pleasant obligations; rather, no matter the obligation, the individual cherishes the value he holds.
For example, parents work hard to send their children

through college. This undertaking is prized even though the hours are long and the work is difficult.

At times, an individual may do something he dislikes in order to achieve and maintain a more important value. Even if dental work is painful, maintaining healthy teeth is more important than the pain. A child does not like helping with the dishes, but one evening he notices that his parents are tired. He suggests that they rest while he finishes the dishes. Instead of feeling annoyed about doing the dishes, the child is pleased and prizes the value of being a real help at home.

Example. Simon, Howe, and Kirschenbaum present a strategy called "Values Whip"[20] to motivate students to realize which values they prize and cherish. The teacher asks a question or makes an open-ended statement. In rapid succession, without thought, students answer the question or complete the statement. If a student were uncertain of the answer or rejected the question, he could pass.

Questions and open-ended statements might include:

    a. What is the one thing you like in your neighborhood?
    b. I recently helped my family by _____.
    c. At school, I am pleased when _____.
    d. Describe situations when adults were helpful and admired.

5. Affirming.

When an individual freely chooses a value, the value is not hidden or ignored. The individual is willing to affirm his value and stand up for it. Whether it is regarding the style or color of a dress or a political alignment or an opinion about a movie or painting, the individual sustains his chosen value alternative. The "affirming" requirement, however, can create a number of problems:

    a. What are the boundaries between public and private life? Are there aspects of a student's or any individual's private life which should not be discussed or open to public scrutiny? The classroom is probably even more of a public forum than the podium of a public assembly. If anything, the same forum of a class or

143

meeting might prove much more intimidating, especially for an adolescent. No matter how a teacher or group leader states that individuals have the right to their own values, adolescents may not heed this statement. During adolescence, youths search for their own unique identity. They imagine what it would be like to accept different values, to live different lives, to travel to distant lands, to run away from home and school, to wear flamboyant clothing and lead dangerous lives. To air these dreams or imaginary values in class may prove difficult.

b. Are these aspects of an individual's private life which should not be discussed in a public forum? The individual himself may prefer that these matters or values remain private. Merely stating that students can pass and do not have to respond to questions or take part in discussion does not resolve the issue. Students may be too embarrassed to refrain from discussing value issues. They may feel that silence indicates a response as clearly as discussion or stated opinion.

Also, there may be aspects of his private life and values which a student may be willing to discuss, but a teacher has no right to explore. This is not a matter of the teacher fearing parental or community pressure or annoyance of the discussion of certain values. More important here is the idea that certain values, problems, and issues perhaps should not be discussed in a public forum.

c. Finally, depending on the student's age, social, and emotional maturity, and past experience, certain values should not be included in values clarification strategies. In other words, before the teacher begins an exercise in values clarification, he would have to decide whether the particular exercise and its value content were valid for the class or group in question.

Basically, the issue here is the teacher or adult being sensitive and aware of students' right to privacy as a basic value. At what point does a values clarification exercise overstep into unacceptable territory? Perhaps the problem can be resolved if the teacher recognizes aspects of his own life he is not willing to discuss, and then can put himself into the place of the students. However, even with these two provisions, considerable care must be taken, especially with younger elementary school children or special-education students.

If a student is quite impressionable, the values presented by others may influence and determine his values. Whether this is valid and worthwhile may well depend on the values in question.

Example. "Public Interview:"[21] With this strategy a student volunteers to be interviewed publicly, e.g., as a public figure would be interviewed on a television program. Simon, Howe, and Kirschenbaum note that the teacher can ask the student any question about his life and values. However, the student may also ask the same questions of the teacher at the end of the interview session. If a student or teacher does not want to answer a question, he can pass. The problem here is that as an adult, the teacher may possess the ability to evade a sensitive question tactfully whereas an adolescent may, instead, become embarrassed.

6. Acting upon Choices.

Too often value or moral education becomes a sophisticated discussion in which individuals present expected or appropriate judgments. Unfortunately, however, there is little effort made for the individual to implement his judgments in action. Obviously, this is a very difficult area, especially for schools. Yet, if value education is to be effective, judgments alone are not sufficient. Judgments need to be manifested in appropriate action. If an individual believes that reading is a vital, enjoyable part of life, then all his leisure time cannot be spent watching television. If exercise is considered an important component of the healthy life, then the individual exercises, whether jogging, playing tennis, golf, or squash, bowling or doing gymnastics. If the individual joins a service organization, the values he cherishes become a part of the way he acts in that situation. A number of proposals for action are possible. Two of them are as follows:

a. Values clarification problems can relate to actual school and student problems with an eye on resolving these problems. In this way, students would not merely discuss and judge, but also would be expected to follow the judgment with suitable action.

b. Students could be involved in various activities and situations which would implement value judgments in practical situations. These might include peer tutoring, being a candy stripe volunteer in a local hospital, working with the elderly, working in various

145

school offices, doing errands for people confined to their homes, and assisting with a Brownie troop. To effect any such values-in-practice movement, the school would have to accept at least a liaison role with various community agencies and organizations.

7. Repeating.

Even though values change or the situations in which values are found changed, the individual needs to possess certain fundamental values, a web of coherent values, which remain throughout life. Values are not changed as an individual daily changes his clothing, but should be repeated in various situations and on different occasions.

In the various books and articles presenting the values clarification strategies and methods, the above seven requirements for value choice or valuation are persistently used.[22] Though many strategies seek to develop skill in one area, some values strategies use a holistic approach and examine a particular value according to all seven categories.

Example. An example of the holistic approach is the values grid.[23] Each values issue, stated by the teacher, is evaluated according to the seven categories.

Such a values issue is:

                                 1 2 3 4 5 6 7
"I watch soap-box operas on television
in the afternoon after school."

(The numbers here refer to the seven categories or requirements of values clarification. Each of these requirements forms a separate question, e.g., (1) have you freely chosen the value? (2) are you proud of your choice or do you prize your choice?, etc. Each question would be answered Y for yes and N for no.)

Someone in the class might ask whether the person who had said he freely chose this value really had. Was the value based on a weighing of the alternatives and consequences, a primary characteristic of free choice? The child might be asked by a classmate whether parents were already watching television when the child arrived home; or, the teacher might ask whether other children in the child's clique watch afternoon television. Concerning alternatives, the teacher might ask the child to enumerate the alternatives which had been considered prior to watching afternoon television.

During values clarification, the teacher has the role of listener and facilitator. He should be non-judgmental, trusting, and accepting of students, their problems, and values. In other words, though the teacher should prod students through questioning and through structuring valid values clarification strategies and issues, the teacher should not make value judgments about which values are most acceptable.

In its present formulation, value clarification by itself remains exceptionally relativistic in that students can accept and choose any conceivable values. Though values clarification assumes students who clarify values will experience positive value growth, there is little attention to even the most generalized formulation of the nature of such growth. Other problems with values clarification still remain, causing an uneasiness for anyone truly concerned with values education and development. First, there is no ordering of moral and non-moral values. Implicit in the content of values clarification strategies is acceptance of the equal importance of all values, moral and non-moral. Actually, advocates of values clarification could present a strong argument for eliminating this distinction, for it could be that this distinction is of limited use in twentieth-century society. For example, if a person has sufficient money, should the desire for luxuries be fully satisfied? The answer may seem obvious. But what if instead of speaking about the single individual, we turn to society in general? At what level does any segment of society have a right to live, especially when the poverty and misfortune of so many is so great? When considered in the light of the poverty-stricken masses of the world, can non-moral values and goods always remain neutral, mere personal predilections and desires? What is still unacceptable is values clarification's inattention to the relative importance of different values. Can the weighting of consequences alone give such ranking?

Second, values clarification stresses that through its strategies, the child develops his own values. If these happen to be the values of the community or parents, all will be delighted. But what if a child accepts destructive values? Is values clarification

147

still insistent that the child himself be the final judge? Obviously, any community or society desires its children to accept its basic values. This is not adequately recognized by values clarification.

Jean Piaget's and Lawrence Kohlberg's theories as presented in the next chapter--contribute the necessary developmental goals and value weighting missing from the values clarification strategies.

NOTES

1. Louis E. Raths, Merrill Harmin, and Sidney B.
Simon, <u>Values</u> <u>and</u> <u>Teaching</u>: Working with Values
in the Classroom (Columbus, Ohio: Charles E. Merrill
Publ. Co., 1966), pp. 5, 6.

2. Raths, Harmin and Simon, <u>op</u>. <u>cit</u>., p. 4.

3. <u>Ibid</u>., p. 5.

4. Howard Kirschenbaum, "Values Education: 1976
and Beyond," <u>The</u> <u>School's</u> <u>Role</u> <u>as</u> <u>Moral</u> <u>Authority</u>,
R. Freeman Butts, et al. (Washington, D. C.:
Association for Supervision and Curriculum Development, 1977), pp. 51-52.

5. <u>Ibid</u>., p. 52.

6. Raths, Harmin and Simon, pp. 28-29.

7. <u>Ibid</u>., pp., 7, 9.

8. William J. Bennett and Edwin J. Delattre, "Moral
Education in the Schools," <u>The</u> <u>Public</u> <u>Interest</u>, vol. 50
(Winter, 1978), pp. 81-98.

9. Alan L. Lockwood, "The Effects of Value Clarification and Moral Development Curricula on School-Age
Subjects: A Critical Review of Recent Research,"
<u>Review</u> <u>of</u> <u>Educational</u> <u>Research</u>, vol. 48 (Summer, 1978),
pp. 33-344.

10. Sidney B. Simon, Leland W. Howe, and Howard
Kirschenbaum, <u>Values</u> <u>Clarification</u>: <u>A</u> <u>Handbook</u>
<u>Strategies</u> <u>for</u> <u>Teachers</u> <u>and</u> <u>Students</u> (New York:
Hart Publishing Co., Inc., 1972), pp. 58-93.

11. Raths, Harmin, and Simon, p. 62.

12. Simon, Howe, and Kirschenbaum, pp. 199-200.

13. Robert T. Hall and John U. Davis, <u>Moral</u> <u>Education</u>
<u>in</u> <u>Theory</u> <u>and</u> <u>Practice</u> (Buffalo, NY.,: Prometheus
Books, 1975), p. 132.

14. Peter McPhail, J. R. Ungoed-Thomas, Hilary
Chapman, Learning to Care (Niles, Ill.: Argus
Communications, 1975), p. 128.

15. Ibid., p. 127.

16. Peter McPhail, J. R. Ungoed-Thomas, Hilary
Chapman, Moral Education in the Secondary School
(London: Longman, 1972), p. 183.

17. Ibid., p. 201.

18. Peter McPhail, J. R. Ungoed-Thomas, Hilary
Chapman, Learning to Care: Rationale and Method
of the Lifeline Program (Niles, Ill.: Argus, 1975),
p. 127.

19. Ibid.

20. Simon, Howe, and Kirschenbaum, pp. 130-138.

21. Ibid., pp. 137-139.

22. In addition to the books already mentioned the
following present additional values clarification
strategies:

(a) Merrill Harmin, Howard Kirschenbaum, Sidney
B. Simon, Clarifying Values Through Subject Matter:
Applications for the Classroom (Minneapolis: Winston
Press, Inc., 1973). This book includes questioning
techniques and the development of value awareness
through movement from a factual level to conceptual
level, and finally to value level in all school
subjects. The final section of the book includes
other values clarification strategies.

(b) Sidney B. Simon and Saly Wendkos Olds, Helping Your Child Learn Right from Wrong: A Guide to
Values Clarification (New York: McGraw-Hill Book Co.,
1977). The game-like strategies in this book were
devised specifically to help parents use values
clarification to assist their children in value
formation.

23. Simon, Howe, and Kirschenbaum, pp. 35-37.

CHAPTER VIII

Values and Personal Autonomy: Piaget and Kohlberg

In a democratic society, brainwashing and indoctrination are usually vehemently castigated as unacceptable methods of educating democratic citizens.[1]
Though conditioning, habit formation, and behavior
modification have been critized by some, these methods
have also been incorporated within the educational
framework of a democratic society. However, few educators or psychologists assume that habitual behavior or
conditioned responses alone are sufficient for individuals to participate fully in a complex, technological
and democratic society. Self-fulfillment and self-
actualization, creativity and happiness, social and
political involvement require higher levels of judgment
and cognition. In contemporary society, individuals
are incessantly bombarded by alluring, attractive
claims, pressures, powers, and goods: the joining of
a cult, club, or lobby, peer group or scholarly group,
the question of whether to keep a promise or tell the
truth, the ability to withstand the charismatic leader
and follow the dictates of one's own conscience. In a
pluralistic society, there are many variations of values
based on a common core of principles and rights. Only
through judgments based on these principles can the
validity of values be determined. Values education in
a pluralistic society must address the problem of autonomous judgments or choices. Habitual behavior and conditioned responses alone cannot furnish the variety of
judgment and responses necessary for all the problems,
values and goods available in contemporary society.
Actually, most moral philosophers claim that the only
fully moral act is the one based on personal, autonomous
moral choice. For example, Niblett expresses this when
he states:

> An individual act is properly to be called
> moral only when a man or woman either de-
> liberately chooses to follow convention in
> spite of temptation to deviate from it, or
> decides not to follow convention but chooses
> instead to do better (or worse) than his
> society tells him to.[2]

Other theoreticians go even further, arguing that an individual act is not moral unless it is based on rational

thought, an autonomous choice, and individually chosen
moral principles.

Instead of concentrating on elementary, simplistic
forms of response and behavior, many psychologists and
educators stress that human development is a principled,
autonomous, and formal stage of moral and value judgment. The individual would be autonomous, judging and
acting dependent on self-chosen moral and value principles and concepts. The individual judges which rules,
standards, ideals or principles are appropriate for particular, unique, concrete moral or value dilemmas.

In 1932, the publication of Jean Piaget's The Moral
Judgment of the Child signaled a new approach to moral
development and the teaching or motivating of principled,
autonomous moral or value judgment. Piaget was not interested in the moral sentiments or actual moral behavior of the child. The child is not viewed as a "little
adult" possessed of all the latent capabilities of
adults, merely awaiting maturation. The moral mind of
the child is also not a blank slate on which society
writes its message. Instead, Piaget asserted that children resolve moral and value dilemmas through different
thought processes than adults. Furthermore, the individual from childhood to adulthood passes through developmental stages, each later stage qualitatively and
logically different from the earlier stage. Empirical
evidence demonstrating the rules, concepts, constraints,
and principles used by children in making moral judgments
were examined by Piaget.

Piaget's method of discovering the principles used
by children was unique compared with the rigorously quantitative and statistical predilections of Anglo-American
psychologists. Piaget's method involves posing moral
dilemmas and through open-ended questioning motivating
children to reveal their thought processes. Piaget is
not merely interested in "what" the child believes is
right or wrong, but "why" the child makes a particular
choice. The "why" furnishes Piaget with the basis for
understanding the child's thought process. Often Piaget
poses two dilemmas and then asks children to compare
their respective moral or non-moral characteristics.
For example, the following two stories were told:

> A. A little boy who is called John is in his
> room. He is called to dinner. He goes into
> the dining room. But behind the door there

was a chair, and on the chair there was
a tray with fifteen cups on it. John
couldn't have known that there was all
this behind the door. He goes in, the
door knocks against the tray, bang go
the fifteen cups and they all get broken!

B. Once there was a little boy whose name
was Henry. One day when his mother was out
he tried to get some jam out of the cup-
board. He climbed up on to a chair and
stretched out his arm. But the jam was
too high up and he couldn't reach it and
have any. But while he was trying to get
it he knocked over a cup. The cup fell
down and broke.[3]

After presenting these stories, two questions were asked: (1) "Are these children equally guilty?! and (2)
"Which of the two is naughtiest and why?! The discussion between the experimenter and the child varies in
length and elaboration. The following is a sample interchange between Roc, age seven, and a psychologist:

"What happens when you tell lies?--You get
punished.--And if you didn't get punished,
would it be naughty to tell them?--No.--
I'm going to tell you two stories. There
were two kiddies and they broke a cup each.
The first one says it wasn't him. His mother
believes him and doesn't punish him. The
second one also says that it wasn't him. But
his mother doesn't believe him and punishes
him. Are both lies that they told equally
naughty?—No.--Which is the naughtiest?--
The one who was punished."[5]

Thus, Roc believes that punishment proves a person's
guilt instead of the more mature logical notion that a
person's action and guilt determines the punishment.

Surprisingly, however, the first hundred pages of
The Moral Judgment of the Child are not devoted to moral
dilemmas of judgments, but to a study of how children
use and judge the rules of games. Piaget finds striking
similarity between the formal constraints of games'
rules and the rules of morality:

(A)ll morality consists in a system of rules,

153

and the essence of all morality is to be
sought for in the respect which the individual acquires for these rules.[6]

Throughout his study and analysis of children's
game rules and their attitudes towards these rules,
Piaget comments about analogous moral concepts. Finally, at the conclusion of this section of the book, he
posits a stage theory of moral judgment development. A
child, according to Piaget, develops from moral realism
and adult constraint to moral autonomy and reciprocity.
The adequacy of this stage theory is then tested by presenting children with moral dilemmas and ascertaining
whether their moral judgments and concomitant justifications follow the posited stages. Piaget expects and
then proves that younger children are in the stage of
moral realism, whereas older children develop to a
morally autonomous and reciprocal stage. Actually, the
lowest and highest stages of moral development represent
two different ways of looking at moral rules. The lower
stage, moral realism, mirrors Durkheim's theory of rules,
externally imposed by societal and parental authority.
Durkheim defines the moral domain in the following passages:

> . . .(T)here is an aspect common to all
> behavior that we ordinarily call moral.
> All such behavior conforms to pre-establish-
> ed rules. To conduct oneself morally is a
> matter of abiding by a norm,. . .[7]

> . . .(W)e can say that morality consists
> of a system of rules of action that pre-
> determine conduct. They state how one <u>must</u>
> act in given situations: . . .[8]

> . . .(M)orality is a totality of definite
> rules; it is like so many molds with limit-
> ing boundaries, into which we <u>must</u> pour our
> behavior.[9]

On the other hand, the highest stage follows Kant's
view of rules as self-imposed and self-determined, based
on rational thought and two categorical imperatives.
Kant's two categorical imperatives are: Each human being
must be viewed as an end, never a means, and each moral
judgment or principle must be universalizable. In
other words, when an agent universalizes a moral judgment, that agent must agree that anyone in a similar

situation can make the same choice and act in the same way.

Before positing the implications of developmental stage theories for formal and informal education, a number of issues need exploration: (a) the nature of autonomy or autonomous judgments; (b) Piaget's theory; and (c) Kohlberg's theory. Finally, the educational implications of these theories will be spelled out.

(a) <u>Autonomy</u> and <u>Autonomous</u> <u>Judgments</u>.

According to the <u>Oxford</u> <u>English</u> <u>Dictionary</u>, autonomy refers to making one's own laws or independence. On the way to understanding autonomy in value judgments, a first approximation of the meaning of autonomy uses these characteristics: An autonomous individual chooses his own values and creates the principles, standards, and rules necessary for resolving value dilemmas. Both with the choice of values and principles or rules, two other ideas are implied:

(i) The choice of values or principles refers to a rational process. Values or principles are not discovered intuitively or given by some external authority. Rather, the individual himself rationally investigates the value dilemma, all possible alternative solutions, the appropriate principles, laws, or rules and the rights of others.

(ii) Choice, in this case, is not dependent upon the individual's immediate emotions or feelings or the possible pleasure or pain he might derive from his choice.

The first approximation seems to suffer a number of failings. A critic might say that it flaunts the facts of actual, concrete value problems, the facts of human life, and the frailties of human beings. After all, human beings are born into particular societies at certain historical periods; their language clamps its own unique restrictions; their families, socio-economic level, and religion contribute to the sum total of an individual's value system. The rules of conduct an individual accepts seems to be consistent with certain rules in social interaction. Rarely are these rules of conduct explicitly or rationally examined. Rather, they are as easily accepted and donned as the scientist puts on his lab coat or the actor his stage make-up and

155

costume. If human beings are prisoners of their society
and family, religion and formal education, profession
and rules, then in what sense are they still autonomous?
Is autonomy a primary myth of the twentieth century, a
myth used to succor and placate the multitudes in technological and democratic societies?

The best that can be said about human value autonomy is that human beings can autonomously choose their
own values, principles, rules, and laws, while staying
within the confines of society, family, language, socio-
economic level, religion, profession, etc. When faced
with innumerable goods and values the individual can
order his priorities, rejecting some values, rationally
choosing others. Even though emotions and feelings remain a motivating force throughout every human life,
and even though an individual may not be able to escape
from his own unique life, autonomy is a realistic, possible option. The autonomous individual transcends and
surmounts the narrow confines of his past and present
concrete life by judging which principles, values, rules,
goods, and laws are valid, universalizable, and rational.

Value and moral problems do not wear their meanings
on their face. There is no sign which states, "this is
a particular type of moral problem" or "this is what
should be done in this case." Ostensibly, it seems the
individual could turn to some authority, such as a
mother, teacher, or spouse, and ask "what should I do?"
However, in this case, it is the mother's, teacher's,
or spouse's moral judgment, not the individual's. The
individual may do the first thing that enters his mind,
acting out of habit; but he has not made a judgment.
He has not chosen. Finally, by accident, the individual
may just happen to resolve what others seem to be a
value or moral problem.

To say that an individual is autonomous or makes
autonomous judgments implies the following conditions:

(i) the individual possesses the means or resources to understand a value dilemma and investigate
the various aspects of the dilemma. This does not imply the absence of research of investigation, but merely that the individual possesses the cognitive abilities necessary for such investigation.

(ii) the individual possesses and applies the
techniques of rational thought in the solution of the

value dilemma.

(iii) the individual asserts what should be done and resolves the problem.

(iv) the individual, by asserting what should be done, is formulating a principle or rule, acceptable in all similar situations faced either by himself or anyone else. All these conditions lead to the idea of the autonomous individual as self-legislating, self-willing, and self-responsible.

(b) Piaget's theory.

Though Piaget believes that the study of individual development, or ontogeny, is valuable in itself, he also claims the inadequacy of studying adult moral or logical development without first studying and understanding children. The problem for psychology cannot be limited to the question, "How does the adult think?" Even the question, "What does the adult think?" or "what is the content or process of adult thought?" is not adequate. Rather, concern must be extended to developmental psychology and the question, "How does the individual develop from early childhood?" Piaget accents the importance of this when he states:

> Child morality throws light on adult morality.
> If we want to form men and women, nothing will
> fit us so well for the task as to study the
> laws that govern their formation.[10]

According to Piaget, children's development through moral stages is universal, sequential, and hierarchical. Development to a higher stage requires the earlier completion of lower stage reasoning, with no necessity, however, that an individual develop to a higher stage. Whether a child develops through the highest stages is dependent on his social milieu, as well as the maturational potentialities inherent in human beings.[11]

Piaget's The Moral Judgment of the Child is the fifth book in what might be described as a constellation of interrelated books studying the development of reasoning in the child. There is parallel development through different cognitive areas. For example, moral realism in children directly parallels the intellectual realism stage.[12]

In the area of moral judgments, the cognitive limitations, abilities, and reasoning of the three-to-
eight year-old child cause him to confuse moral rules
and physical rules, which are fixed and eternal. Human
intentions, purposes, values and needs do not enter the
child's evaluation. At this stage of moral realism,
the young child views rules as possessing "a sacred
reality."[13] They are considered absolute, unchanging
and unchangeable, and parents are considered omnipotent.
Whatever the parental rule, or punishment, it is considered fair, merely by virtue of the parent's omni-
potence. At this stage, there is belief in immanent
justice--the idea that nature itself punishes misdeeds.
"The child having acquired, thanks to adult restraint,
the habit of punishment attributes spontaneously to
nature the power of applying the same punishments."[14]
For example, a child might believe that nightmares are
punishments for misdeeds.[15]

At the moral realism stage, children believe in re-
tributive justice instead of distributive justice, in
expiatory justice rather than equitable justice. In
other words, the child postulates an objective rather
than subjective form of wrongdoing, accepting the letter
rather than the spirit of the law. Shades of grey are
non-existent at the lower stage, with the purposes and
intentions of the agent ignored and the actual consequences of the action being the deciding factor. For
example, the following are interpretations of Piaget's
earlier-stated two-cup stories. A six year old child
is asked:

> Are these children both naughty, or is
> one not so naughty as the other?--Both
> just as naughty.[16]

In response to the question of whether he would punish
both in the same manner, the child responds that he
would inflict greater punishment on the one who broke
more cups. In other words, the child does not even
consider that in one case breakage was accidental and
in the other, caused by "stealing."

Another six year old not only would punish the hy-
pothetical child of the story, but responds in a similar way when the experimenter changes the situation
slightly by asking:

. . .If it was you who had broken the
twelve cups when you went into the room
and your little sister who had broken one
cup while she was trying to get the jam,
which of you would be punished most
severely?--<u>Me</u>, <u>because</u> <u>I</u> <u>broke</u> <u>more</u>
<u>than</u> <u>one</u> <u>cup</u>."[17]

After eight or nine years, the child becomes more
relativistic. There is movement toward reciprocity and
equity in value and moral judgments and in the evaluation of punishment. The idea of immanent justice de-
creases. In terms of authority, parents and adults
are no longer viewed as omnipotent; rather, judgments
are assessed in relativistic terms and on the basis
of right or wrong for a given situation. Finally, instead of only considering the consequences of action,
the intentions or purposes of the moral agent become
the primary factor deciding the goodness or badness of
action.

To summarize Piaget's moral developmental stages:
The first stage, moral realism, lasting until the child
is seven or eight has "justice . . .subordinated to adult
authority."[18] Between eight and eleven, the child enters
a boundary region, accepting greater relativity and
equity in moral judgments. Then, at about eleven or
twelve, there develops a "purely equalitarian justice.
. .tempered by considerations of equity."[19] Here the
child moves from pure heteronomy to autonomy, in which
his cognitive ability to differentiate situations allows
him to perceive the actual features of moral dilemmas.[20]
Piaget described moral autonomy and the movement from
moral realism or heteronomy to moral autonomy in the
following passages:

Nothing could be truer than to say that
autonomy presupposes a scientific knowledge of social as of natural laws and
the ability to recognize these laws at
work. But social laws are unfinished
and their progressive formation presup-
poses <u>the</u> <u>unfettered</u> <u>cooperation</u> <u>of</u> <u>per-</u>
<u>sonal</u> <u>reason</u>. The autonomy of reason has
. . . nothing to do with individual fancy.[21]

. . . cooperation suppresses both egocentrism and moral realism, and thus achieves
an interiorization of rules. A new morality

follows upon that of pure duty. Heteronomy
steps aside to make way for a consciousness
of good, of which autonomy results from the
acceptance of the norms of reciprocity.
Obedience withdraws in favour of the idea
of justice and of mutual service, now the
source of all obligations which til then had
been imposed as incomprehensible commands.[22]

The years immediately following the development of
Piaget's provocative theory were a period of relative
disinterest in that theory. From 1932 to 1958 primarily
replicative studies examined such problems as whether
socio-economic level, cultural background, parental
child raising practices, IQ, language style, and peer
group relations affected the various dimensions of
Piaget's theory. Thus, for twenty-five years, while
the remainder of Piaget's early works gained disciples,
except for these replicative studies, his moral development theory remained relatively dormant and had little
practical implication for education.

(c) Kohlberg's Theory.[23]

In 1958, Lawrence Kohlberg, in his doctoral dis-
sertation, planted Piaget's moral developmental theory
in uniquely American soil by restructuring Piaget's
original theory. Kohlberg's theoretical proposal was
nourished by his own empirical studies. Following
Piaget's lead, Kohlberg ascertained an individual's
stage of moral development by presenting a moral dilemma and open-ended questioning to determine the principles used and the processes of thought. For example,
the following is one of the dilemmas presented.

In Europe, a woman was near death from a
special kind of cancer. There was only
one drug that the doctors thought might
save her. It was a form of radium that a
druggist in the same town had recently
discovered. The drug was expensive to
make, but the druggist was charging ten
times what the drug cost him to make. He
paid $200 for the radium and charged $2,000
for a small dose of the drug. The sick
woman's husband, Heinz, went to everyone
he knew to borrow the money, but he could
only get together about $1,000, which is
half of what it cost. He told the druggist

160

that his wife was dying and asked him to
sell it cheaper, or let him pay later.
But the druggist said, "No, I discovered
the drug and I'm going to make money from
it." So Heinz got desperate and broke into
the man's store to steal the drug for his wife.

Should Heinz have done that? Was it actually
wrong or right? Why?[24]

Depending on the answers to these and various other
questions and to other moral dilemmas, the individual's
moral cognitive stages of development are determined.

Each story is a moral dilemma since each presents
a moral conflict. In the Heinz dilemma, the conflict
is between the druggist's right of property and the
wife's right to life. There are other conflicts in
this story as well. For example, the individual re-
spondent determines whether right or wrong refers to
the legal or the moral domain. Kohlberg assumes that
individuals interpret moral dilemmas, even adding material not actually given in the original dilemma, dependent on their achieved developmental stage. By studying these characteristics of practical reasoning, Kohlberg disdains interest in simple "yes" or "no" responses to moral dilemmas. Instead, the important responses
are the justifications, the interpretations of concepts
and ideas, and the reasons for one's moral choice, since
these indicate the individual's developmental stage.

Is this interest in moral development stages merely
an intellectual or scholarly curiosity? What practical
implications does knowledge of such stage theory have
for the average person? Kohlberg assumes that moral or
value education requires some aim. What type of behavior, judgments, and values is education aiming toward?
If an individual's potential for development and education is to a higher level, teachers and parents have
the responsibility to motivate such developments.
Kohlberg argues that an individual at higher stages or
levels of development can do things and make judgments
not possible at a lower stage; therefore, both the individual and society benefit from the individual's
greater development.

In his theory Kohlberg posits two types of structure or form which universally support and give order

161

and meaning to the moral life of societies and human beings.

(1) First, Kohlberg posits 26 moral categories universally underlying all moral concerns: eight modes of judgment of obligation and value, seven elements of obligation and value, and eleven issues or institutions. If the concrete, particular moral situations, institutions, concerns, and mores of each society are categorized or structured in general form, Kohlberg expects these twenty-six categories will be discerned. If Kohlberg's theory were limited to the discovery of these twenty-six categories of moral life, it would have little impact, for philosophers, sociologists, and anthropoligists have long studied common categories or concerns underlying the moral life of all human beings. However, in the past, most thinkers assumed that different societies and groups at different historical periods and in different places posited radically different solutions to identical moral problems. Kohlberg states that every society is concerned with human life. Is this really true? Contemporary western society claims each human being's inalienable right to life. Other societies, such as those of the eskimo and bushman, do not seem to recognize this right. The elderly or enfeebled voluntarily leave their society to guarantee the life of others. Whether or not the eskimo or bushman societies actually value life in the same manner as Western society is unimportant, for Kohlberg's category "the value of life" is not damaged by differences between societies. Kohlberg only asserts that universally every society is concerned with the problem of life as a moral category or issue. He does not state what position should be accepted by any society or individual. How individuals and societies actually judge such an issue will be determined by their developmental stage of moral cognitive judgments.

(2) The second part of Kohlberg's theory sets him apart from previous theoreticians and contributes to the theory's novelty and suggestiveness. Kohlberg posits three levels, each of which is subdivided into two stages, thus giving six stages of moral cognitive development as compared to Piaget's three stages. Kohlberg's six stages are asserted to be invariant, sequential, universal, and hierarchical. Following Piaget's assumptions, Kohlberg is not primarily interested in moral behavior or sentiments, but concentrates on the process of moral thought or judgments and the evolution of moral

162

judgmental stages. With each different sequential stage, an individual interprets moral dilemmas and the previously mentioned 26 moral concerns from a different perspective, using a different structure of thought. By positing a hierarchical sequence of six moral stages, Kohlberg asserts that at each stage, the individual judges moral dilemmas and uses moral discourse, organizes his thought and uses principles through the perspective of whichever moral developmental stage or level has been achieved. Stages are "total ways of thinking, not attitudes toward particular situations."[25]

Before proceeding to a description of the stages, it would be helpful to understand Kohlberg's characterization of stages as universal, invariant, sequential, and hierarchical.

(a) First, stages are universal in that all human beings in every society develop through these stages. This does not require an individual or society to reach the highest stage(s). Moral development can cease at any stage. Kohlberg does not merely assume his theory is universally valid, but attempts to demonstrate this through empirical evidence derived from cross-cultural studies in Mexico, Taiwan, Turkey, Israel, etc. In each different society, Kohlberg developed moral dilemmas appropriate for the particular cultural milieu. For example, instead of the Heinz dilemma, noted previously, in Taiwan Kohlberg substituted the following story:

> A man and wife had just migrated from the
> high mountains. They started to farm, but
> there was no rain, and no crops grew. No
> one had enough food. The wife got sick,
> and finally she was close to dying from having
> no food. There was only one grocery store in
> the village, and the storekeeper charged a
> very high price for the food. The husband
> asked the storekeeper for some food for his
> wife, and said he would pay for it later.
> The storekeeper siad, "No, I won't give you
> any food unless you pay first." The husband
> went to all the people in the village to ask
> for food, but no one had food to spare. So
> he got desperate and broke into the store to
> steal food for his wife.

Should the husband have done that? Why?[26]
Even a superficial comparison of this story with the
Heinz dilemma reveals that the form of both dilemmas
is quite similar with the basic conflict being between
the right of property (the druggist or grocery-store
owner) and the right to life (the women). The univer-
sality of stages has been demonstrated empirically not
merely for different societies, but for different groups
in the United States; that is, different socio-economic
levels and different ethnic and religious groups.

(b) Kohlberg believes that stages are unvariant
and sequential. This refers to the idea that a child
must move through the six stages, stage by stage. Any
individual may become fixated at a lower stage and different individuals move through the developmental stages
at varying rates, but if an individual moves to a higher stage, he must first have developed through the necessary lower stages. He cannot skip stages or change
the order of stages.

Moral development is neither an inner unfolding
occurring automatically nor an imprinting on a passive
blank slate by external stimuli. Rather, development
is based on interaction between the individual's present cognitive structures and the external social environment; that is, between the individual's stage of
reasoning and other human beings. Furthermore, paral-
lelism between appropriate cognitive logical stages,
ego or social stages, and moral stages is assumed. In
other words, besides the necessity of completing development in the adjacent lower moral development stage,
the individual also must previously have completed adequate development in parallel Piagetean logical cognitive stages and have resolved crises in the appropriate
parallel Erikson eight stages of ego development.

(c) Moral development is irreversible. Though
considered irreversible, Kohlberg qualified this with
the expression "usually irreversible." Kohlberg's use
of the word "usually" indicates one possible thorn in
his theory. One of Kohlberg's empirical studies examines a women's prison before and after implementation
of Kohlberg's "just" cottage community. For our purposes the "before" is especially relevant. Before beginning the experiment, the moral development stages of
these women was determined, based on their responses to
moral dilemmas concerning both prison life and civilian
life. Though the women scored at stages 3 or 4 in their

164

responses to civilian moral dilemmas such as the Heinz
dilemma, they only scored at stage 1 or 2 on prison
moral dilemmas. In other words, using Kohlberg's
terminology, there was slippage or regression from
higher stages to lower stages over a period of time.[27]

(d) Finally, the hierarchical stage refers to the
idea that lower stages exist for a number of logical
reasons: (i)They are necessary conditions for movement
to the next higher stage. (ii) The characteristics of
the lower-stage judgment lack the differentiation and
synthesis possible at a higher stage.

The three Kohlberg moral levels can be described
not only as involving six different structures of moral
thought but as increasing awareness and understanding
of moral life, principles, and judgments. For example,
the three moral levels can be described as concentric
circles of increasing radius. The inner circles are
the pre-conventional levels in which the child deals
with pleasure versus pain, good versus evil, obedience
versus badness, favors versus punishment. At this level,
the individual cannot take the role of others, does not
internalize particular rules, and perceives adults as
unquestioned authorities. The middle circles are the
conventional levels and represent the enlarging world
of the individual. The child has moved out of his immediate family and a narrow social domain and through
interaction begins to recognize and accept the rights
of others. At this conventional level, the individual
not only accepts the demands, values, rules, morality
of his family, peer group, religion, ethnic group, but
actively seeks to propagate these. The outer circles
represent the post-conventional stages in which the individual internalizes moral principles and recognizes
himself as an autonomous individual capable of making
principled, universalizable moral judgments.

Kohlberg asserts that only the higher moral stages,
stages 5 and 6, are fully moral, since only at these
stages are individuals autonomously judging moral problems. In the next sections, the characteristics of
the three levels and six stages are described, indicating the movement from egocentrism and external authority to autonomous, principled moral judgments. Before
looking at the moral stages of development, it is worth
stressing again that as with Piaget, Kohlberg is not
concerned with the content of the response. In other
words, he does not care whether an individual believes

Heinz should or should not steal the drug for his wife. Rather, Kohlberg is concerned <u>only</u> with the <u>form</u> or <u>structure</u> of the moral judgment. Kohlberg is interested in answers to the following questions: What is the process of moral thought? What justification does the individual use when developing his moral judgment?

<u>Moral</u> <u>Cognitive</u> <u>Structures</u>:

<u>Preconventional</u> <u>Level</u>

The lowest level, the preconventional level includes two stages: stage 1, punishment and obedience orientation; and stage 2, the instrumental relativist orientation. The following general characteristics describe the preconventional level as a whole: The individual accepts society's or his mother's or father's labels of right, bad, good, or wrong. However, these labels are interpreted by the child only in terms of physical or exceptionally hedonistic consequences of action. In particular, punishment, especially physical punishment and the immediacy of punishment, determine whether behavior is considered good or bad. In other words, if someone is punished for something he did not do, the person is considered bad or guilty, merely because of the punishment. In addition, favour exchanges and rewards are considered important. Considerations of punishment, reward, favour exchanges or the goodness, evil, rightness or badness of behavior tend to be arbitrary and absolute.

Women prisoners' assumption that prison justice was at the preconventional stage was based on the arbitrary, unquestioning nature of the prison system. There was no rhyme or reason to judgments of the rightness or wrongness of actions or the character of punishments in the minds of prisoners.[28]

<u>Stage</u> <u>1</u>: The <u>Punishment</u> <u>and</u> <u>Obedience</u> <u>Orientation</u>.

At this stage the individual faces punishment, fears punishment, and accepts the rules and dictates of those who have the power to inflict punishment. The idea of a moral code is foreign to stage 1 thought processes or reasoning. Since the stage 1 individual is concerned with the immediacy of punishment, the severity of punishment, and the power of authorities, the moral is inherently connected with these qualities.

When responding to the Heinz dilemma, the stage 1 individual bases his judgment on the consequences, the punishment resulting from stealing. A human being's right to life is unimportant. Even more surprising is his response to the question, "If you were dying, but still had the strength to steal the drug, would you steal it?" The stage 1 individual would very probably say, "no!", for even if he took the drug, he would be put in jail and die anyway.

At this lowest stage, the individual cannot differentiate between human beings and artifact. Thus, a child might not see any difference between the death of the woman and the destruction of furniture. An example of this occurs in Charles Dickens' Dombey and Son:

> To record of Mr. Dombey that he was not in
> his way affected by this . . . (knowledge
> of the possibility of his wife's death)
> would be to do him an injustice. He was
> not a man of whom it could properly be
> said that he was ever startled or shocked;
> but he certainly had a sense within him that
> if his wife should sicken and decay, he would
> be very sorry, and that he would find a some-
> thing gone from among his plate and furni-
> ture, and other household possessions, which
> was well worth the having, and could not be
> lost without sincere regret.[29]

Stage 2:   The Instrumental Relativist Orientation.

At stage 2, an individual interprets right action as whatever satisfies or contributes to the satisfaction of his own needs, interests, or pleasure. Another individual's needs or interests are satisfied according to the "you scratch my back and I'll scratch yours" principle. The "moral" agent reciprocates not because of loyalty, fairness, gratitude, friendship, the inherent worth of human beings, or blood relationship. Rather, a stage 2 individual wants to insure the other's conduct towards him, when he is in need. Thus, someone at stage 2 would believe that Heinz should steal the drug, but only because a husband needs his wife. After all, a wife does the cooking, cleaning, and mending. Therefore, there is a trade; the husband steals the drug to insure the wife's continued services. The exchange issue is paramount when the stage 2 individual

is asked, "What if Heinz does not feel particularly af-
fectionate towards his wife, should he still steal the
drug?" A stage 2 high school student responded, "If
he's having an affair with someone else who will cook
and clean for him, then he doesn't have to steal the
drug for his wife."

Responses from the cross-cultural study using the
starving wife story, stress the justification and reasoning of the stage 2 individual. For example, stage 2
children in Taiwan responded in the following way:

He should steal the food for his wife,
because if she dies he'll have to pay
for her funeral and that costs a lot.

He should steal the food because he
needs his wife to cook for him.

In the first instance, the response is based on what
contributes to the husband's interests, not paying for
an expensive funeral. In the second, the major stress
is favour-exchange.

The Conventional Level

At this level, there is movement away from concern
with the immediate, physical consequences of an action.
Whether an action is consistent with a particular accepted moral code becomes important. At the conventional level, the individual attempts to maintain the expectations, values, mores, customs, rules, code of his
family, peer group, ethnic group, religion, or nation.

Stage 3: The Interpersonal Concordance of "good boy-nice girl"

Orientation.

At stage 3, the individual attempts to maintain behavior that will please and help others and be approved
by them. In other words, the individual conforms with
the stereotypes of the majority, what the majority considers "natural" or "normal" behavior.

Kohlberg interprets the frequently-used expression
at this stage, "he means well," as indicating the beginning use of intention to judge the goodness or badness
of actions. At this stage, action is ". . . motivated

by anticipation of disapproval from punishment, fear, or pain.[31] The following responses indicate the stage 3 motives for moral action, though each response takes an opposing viewpoint: Pro-that Heinz should steal the drug:

> No one will think you're bad if you steal the drug, but your family will think that you're an inhuman husband if you don't. If you let your wife die, you'll never be able to look anybody in the face again.[32]

Con-that Heinz should not steal the drug:

> It isn't just the druggist who will think you're a criminal, everyone else will too. After you steal it, you'll feel bad thinking how you've bought dishonor on your family and yourself; you won't be able to face anyone again.[33]

Stage 4: Law and Order Orientation.

At stage 4, the individual accepts legal authority, fixed rules, and the maintenance of the social order. "Right behavior consists of doing one's duty, showing respect for authority, and maintaining the given social order for its own sake.[34] Though the stage 4 individual sympathizes with Heinz's dilemma, he often believes that adherence to the approved and legal order and the system of rules and laws must take precedence over Heinz's personal desires. If Heinz were to waver in his allegiance to nation and the laws, in stage 4 individual's judgment, chaos or anarchy could result. Following this line of reasoning, the stage 4 individual might respond in the following to the Heinz dilemma:

> No, Heinz shouldn't have done that. It was wrong because he was breaking the law no matter how you look at it and, although I can see why he would have done it, I don't think he was justified in doing it. If he would have thought long and hard enough, he could have come up with an alternative because there is always an alternative. I agree with his intent but not his method. (Maybe he could have gotten a government loan or something.)[35]

When asked whether Heinz should be punished if he steals the drug, the stage 4 individual states that "he must be punished to keep our system running smoothly." From this last statement, the basic orientation of a stage 4 individual is apparent. A "law and order" individual speaks of the "good American," the average citizen who must follow the law, no matter its demands. Though democracy is based on majority rule, in constitutional democracy protection of minority rights is equally important. For the stage 4 individual, minority rights are pushed into the background, with majority rights and rule or "general will" becoming a sacred entity, to be unquestioningly accepted and followed.

The weaknesses of stage 4 moral reasoning are stressed by Kohlberg: (1) First, there is no way to define obligations to or the rights of individuals outside of one's own "law and order" system. In other words, is it really possible to determine one's moral responsibilities or duty to citizens of another country by using the laws of one's own country? (ii) Second, problems of how to interpret laws or mores cannot be adjudicated merely by recourse to this stage. Often, interpretation of particular laws or customs or mores depends on the realm of commonly held beliefs, not on reasoned justification of the interpretation. Such interpretation of laws needs some standards and principles outside of the laws themselves. This fact is apparent when one looks at the changing interpretations of the Supreme Court.

(iii) Finally, laws in themselves do not present guidelines for social reform or change. There is no method for creating new laws or norms. In fact, there is no way of judging the adequacy or validity of the current laws or norms themselves. No matter how adequate, fair, and just the laws of any country seem at one particular period, at another time, they become obsolete and require change.

Many ugly forms of stage 4 conventional morality have arisen in human history. One might cite Nazi Germany as an example of a country with a stage 4 morality.

The Postconventional, Autonomous Level.

For Kohlberg, only this level is a fully moral level. For at other levels and stages the individual judges and reasons according to external pressures,

constraints, laws, rules, norms, or customs. For example, an individual's own desires and emotions, the
mores and whims of family and friends, authorities and
marketplace relationships all determine moral reasoning at the lower levels. Only at the post-conventional level does the individual himself define values,
moral concepts, and principles apart from the groups
and persons holding those values or principles.

Stage 5: The Social Contract Legalistic Orientation.

Kohlberg claims that this stage possesses utilitari-
an overtones, i.e., consideration of the principle, the
greatest happiness for the greatest number. Not only
is the individual concerned with the legal rule as de-
mocratically determined, but also free agreements and
contracts possessing binding obligation. Right action
is understood as relating to general individual rights
and standards which have been critically examined and
agreed upon by the whole of society. "There is a clear
awareness of the relativism of personal values and opinions and corresponding emphasis upon procedural rules
for reaching consensus."[36]

At this stage, an individual might give the following response to the Heinz dilemma:

> There is a moral conflict here. It is
> wrong for Heinz to steal the drug--it
> is not his. But it would be more wrong
> for Heinz to let his wife die. Thus,
> although Heinz is not _right_ or _justified_
> in stealing the drug, he is _more_ right
> and _more_ justified than if he had let her
> die.[37]

Kohlberg states that "the core development of stage 5
is the elaboration of a 'rational' approach to making
laws or rules, a law-making perspective which is clearly distinguished from the law-maintaining perspective.[38]
Thus, constitutional conventions such as the ones of the
Founding Fathers, and the legislative procedures of the
American Congress would be example of this "law-making
perspective." On a more simplistic level, an elementary school teacher who had his students discuss and
determine class rules, would be implementing stage 5
procedures. The students would not merely be maintaining rules, but would be making them.

Kohlberg further described this lawmaking stage 5 in the following way:

> When we turn to stage 5 procedural rules for lawmaking, we find that they all invoke one or another element of the contract notion. This social-contract notion is a procedural legislative principle which presupposes that both the obeyer of the law and the lawmaker have the proper orientation, and that the lawmaker has received the rational consent of the individuals composing society . . . .

> The social-contract which is the basis of the stage 5 socio-moral order is a justice conception which presupposes reciprocity of the partners to the agreement and equality between them prior to the agreement.[39]

Stage 6: The Universal Ethical Principle Orientation.

In his summary of stage 6, Kohlberg states:

> Right is defined by the decision of conscience in accord with self-chosen ethical principles appealing to logical comprehensiveness, universality, and consistency. These principles are abstract and ethical (the Golden Rule, the categorical imperative); they are not concrete moral rules like the Ten Commandments. At heart, these are universal principles of justice, of the reciprocity and equality of human rights, and of respect for the dignity of human beings as individual persons (Kohlberg's italics).[40]

To distinguish between stage 5 and stage 6 and to demonstrate that stage 6 is logically and morally more adequate than stage 5, Kohlberg quotes the response of two philosophers to the Heinz dilemma. Philosopher 1 would be designated at stage 5, whereas philosopher 2 is at stage 6.

> Philosopher 1: What Heinz did was not wrong. The distribution of scarce drugs should be regulated by principles of fairness. In the absence of such regulation, the druggist was within his legal rights, but in the circumstances he has no moral complaint. He

172

still was within his moral rights, however,
unless it was within his society a strongly
disapproved thing to do. While what Heinz
did was not wrong, it was not his duty to
do it. The crucial questions are (1) Does
the wife (or friend) have a right to the
drug? (2) Does the druggist have a right to
withhold the drug? (3) Does Heinz have a
duty to help his wife (or friend)? In this
case it is not wrong for Heinz to steal the
drug but it goes beyond the call of duty,
it is a deed of supererogation.[41]

On the other hand, philosopher 2 replied to the question
of whether Heinz should steal the drug in the following
manner:

Yes, it was wrong legally, but right morally.
I believe that one has at least a prima
facie duty to save a life . . ., and in this
case, the legal duty not to steal is clearly
outweighted by the moral duty to save a life.

It is my belief that systems of law are valid,
only insofar as they reflect or embody the
sort of moral law which most rational men
recognize and all rational men can accept.

In the case of conflict between the imperative of a specific law and a moral imperative,
one can often "see" or intuit that one "ought"
to break a law in order to fulfill a moral
duty.[42]

The differences between these two responses clearly indicate the differences between stage 5 and stage 6.
With the stage 5 response, there is a strong basis of
social contract and the claims of laws which have been
arrived at by mutual consent. With stage 6, there
is a stress on the sanctity of human life and the overwhelming importance of individual conscience and personal, rational choice of moral principles. In the full
responses of the respective philosophers, one discerns
other differences. (i) Though the stage 5 person accepted that Heinz should steal the drug, there was no
obligation to do so. The stage 6 individual accepted
that Heinz had an obligation, a duty. (ii) The resolution of the tension between legal and moral obligation
is left fairly ambiguous for the stage 5 individual,

whereas the stage 6 individual clearly enunciates the
priority of the moral duty over the legal one.

The Implications of Piaget's and Kohlberg's Theories
for Moral Education.

   Cognitive developmental psychologists like Piaget
and Kohlberg avoid the use of such terms as "teaching"
or "preaching" and criticize theories which advocate
either indoctrination or socialization.[43] Instead,
they stress the ideal of motivating development. In
this section, methods of motivating or catalyzing moral
development to higher stages are explored.

Discussion and Dialogue concerning Value and Moral
Problems.

   In the home, community, and school, parents,
adults, or authorities might command allegiance to certain values and might tell others what to do in specific
situations. Besides being ineffective, such methods do
not allow for the moral development of either member of
the social interchange, either the person giving orders
or the person obeying the orders. Dialogue and discussion concerning the resolution of value or moral
conflicts would motivate the moral development of all
individuals involved in the dialogue. During such
dialogue and discussion, the individual not only gives
reasons and examines his reasons for advocating a particular choice, but also comes into contact with the
reasoning and principles of other individuals.

   Other people's reasoning, judgments, and principles
would create cognitive dissonance for people at lower
moral judgmental levels. Cognitive dissonance refers
to two or more ideas or elements not fitting in or
meshing with each other. These elements may be contradictory or inconsistent; they may not fit with accepted group, personal, or society standards.[44] For example,
an individual may strengthen his decision to purchase a
particular make or model car by reading advertisements
and articles showing the practicality of aesthetic quality of his decision. He might consult experts, e.g.,
favorable assessments of the car in Road and Track or
Consumer Reports. However, if someone tells him about
the number of "lemons" produced, the many mechanical and
production faults in the car, about its great consumption of gas and oil, or about difficulties in repairing

174

the car, the individual experiences cognitive dissonance. Whereas previously he was certain of his decision, he is now confused, uncertain, or upset. He wonders if his original decision was the correct one. Perhaps, he should not buy the originally chosen model, but retain his old car or choose a different model.

A discussion of a moral dilemma, should not merely be an unorganized, freewheeling, or chaotic affair, with each individual attempting to convert others to his point of view. Discussion of moral dilemmas should not include persuasion through an individual's personality, emotional devices, rhetoric, chicanery, or position of authority. Rather, the organization of the discussion is of the utmost importance to insure its validity and rationality. The following are a number of suggestions for guiding such discussions:

1. What is the value or moral problem? How is the value or moral problem selected? The range of value or moral problems that could be discussed is great:

(a) An actual personal problem. The problem may be an actual problem for a child, parent, teacher, community social worker, or club member. Often, adults remind children about moral problems. However, these are problems perceived and accepted by the adults. For the child these problems may exist only because some authority figure insists that they do. The child may not really care about the problem. A British moral development project attempts to avoid this problem by using dilemmas students themselves perceive. Before actually constructing a moral education curriculum, McPhail, Ungoed-Thomas, and Chapman asked adolescents to cite examples of commendable, helpful and reasonable adult behavior. The adolescent students were also asked to identify situations in which adults were unreasonable, hostile, and overly critical. From adolescent responses to these and other questions, the authors created situations used in the "Lifeline" moral educational curriculum. The moral dilemmas used reflected the actual moral concerns of adolescents.[45]

Similarly, discussion in a home could include moral problems with which children are actually concerned. In addition, adults could give children insight into the moral problems which the adults find particularly pressing or difficult. Here, of course, the structuring of the problem would depend on the child's age. It is infrequent that adults confide in children, allowing the child to know that parents are not all-powerful or problem-free, that adults as well as children must resolve moral problems. Children and adolescents gain knowledge about the process and standards or making value or moral judgments if adults are willing to share and discuss adult problems and decision-making processes.

(b) Actual Problems from Other Sources.

Actual problems can also include those presented in newspapers, magazines, literature, or on television. Situations in other countries, political behavior or misbehavior, social inequities, plays, mysteries, legal battles, biomedical cases, and business decisions can become the basis for discussions. Often families watch television and comment on the news or read newspapers and superficially note an attitude regarding a particular event. Such offhand comment or the silent presentation of facts on television does little, if anything, to engender moral development.

At times, a child may wonder about some value or moral problem she has seen on television. Or she may not fully understand a values problem parents are discussing. In the natural setting of the home, a parent can engender discussion with a child, asking whether the child agrees with the decision made in some situation or why he believes someone made a particular decision. Of particular importance would be the reasons and principles the child notes. In other words, it is not sufficient for the child to say, "I wouldn't do that" or "He should go to jail." Rather, through discussion, questioning, and rational interchange, adults should motivate the child to reveal his reasoning. It would be especially important for the adult to remain nonjudgmental, not telling the child what she should think or believe. Rather, the parent should accept the child's ideas, recognizing that they are the ideas of a child at a particular developmental stage.

Situations from current events and the rich heritage of literature provide some of the most natural and interesting material for moral education. Though considerable artificially constructed and contrived moral education curriculums have been "packaged in glossy covers and sold in school, (these) are at best second to the quarry of moral explications and moral narrative available to teachers and known as the corpus of

the humanities."[46] At all educational levels and for all
stages of development literature possesses appropriate
examples. Even if the aesthetic component is the important or primary one when reading books, moral or
value problems can also be derived from these sources,[47]

(c) _Artificial_ _Problems_. A teacher or parent may
decide to present or discuss an imaginary or hypotheti-
cal problem, choosing either a "cold" problem or a "hot"
problem. A hot problem would be a problem with which
students would be emotionally involved. For example, an
imaginary problem about a star football player's dismissal (or suspension) from the team for some school
rule infraction might be a "hot" problem for students
emotionally involved with their school football team.
Even if this problem were presented as an imaginary or
artificial problem, it might prove too close to the
climate of the class, especially if a very similar situation had recently occurred in the school.

This is not to say that "hot" problems should never
be used. One way of introducing a "hot" problem would
be through prior study of a similar "cold" problem. For
example, perhaps an artificial problem involving an
athlete from Ancient Greece could spark discussion. The
distance between this problem and students would allow
for rational, objective investigation and resolution of
the problem. Only then, might a "hot" problem be discussed, with the earlier "cold" problem serving as an
example.

2. _What_ _is_ _the_ _correct_, _valid_, _or_ _objective_ _state-_
ment _of_ _the_ _dilemma_? In his writings on reflective
thinking and problem solving, John Dewey stressed the
importance of identifying, intellectualizing, or stating
the problem. Merely a feeling that a problem exists is
not sufficient. The individual must know what the problem actually is.

Most often, the way an individual intellectualizes
a problem suggests that person's moral development
stage. For example, the individual at lower stages of
moral development might view the Heinz dilemma only
through a legalistic framework. The very nature of the
person's analysis of the dilemma indicates an inability
to think at the higher stages.

Example. A parent may be very annoyed at something
that happened. This annoyance may be conveyed to a
child through the tone of the question, "what did you do?"

177

In addition, the scowl on the parent's face might betray
his anger. The child may begin to tremble or cry, may
begin to make excuses or become truculent; however, this
does not mean that the child knows what the parent is
questioning or what the problem is. Even if a parent
asks a child why he lied, the child may not understand
the problem, for the child may not know what it means
to lie. The child may not know in what situation lying
took place. Of course, the child probably recognizes
that the parent is accusing him of doing something
wrong, the parent is angry and that the parent's anger
is plainly against the child. Even if a child recognizes a problem, he may stress one aspect of the problem,
whereas a parent may stress a different aspect.

The difficulty of understanding a value or moral
dilemma is not confined to the young child. Adolescents and adults often selectively interpret a problem depending upon their beliefs, intellectual skills,
and emotional involvement with different issues. For
example, when questioned about whether Heinz should
steal the drug to save his wife, many students say,
"Yes! Heinz should steal the drug. After all, he loves
his wife." Then it is pointed out that the dilemma
does not state that Heinz loves his wife. However, some
of these students claim that, "Heinz would not be married if he were not in love." Other students claim
that Heinz would not have tried so hard to get the drug
if he did not love his wife. The students' own beliefs
determined how they interpreted the Heinz dilemma,
what they added and omitted.

Though the nature of the value or moral dilemma may
evolve during the discussion, with new elements and interpretation constantly being presented, any rational
discussion of value or moral dilemmas requires a clear,
objective statement of the problem.

(3) Reasons are developed for accepting the various
alternatives (and their consequences). One expectation
of moral and value education is that individuals will be
able to make their own judgments. They will not blind-
ly and unthinkingly follow some external authority.
Their value and moral judgments are based on rational,
reasoned thought processes, on their own determination
of which is the best judgment and course of action.
Basic to the entire Piaget and Kohlberg moral development theories is the idea that at each stage the individual uses different reasons and principles for the judgments made. Any attempt to determine an individual's

178

moral stage or to motivate further moral development, therefore, necessitates the individual revealing the reasons and principles underlying his judgment. When these reasons or principles are presented in a discussion, other students may disagree with the reasons, argue against them, or strengthen them. In all probability, a few students may accept similar reasons, with other students disagreeing with the reasons.

Adolescents, especially, challenge rules, whether societal, school, or parental rules. Some rules are rational and their demise would spell the demise of humane and considerate interpersonal relationships. However, the soundness or rational nature of a rule to an adult does not imply that an adolescent should not question, examine, and prove the validity or unacceptability of social rules, for it is through such personal examination and acceptance that a rule which was external to the adolescent can become internalized.

While Kohlberg merely stresses the use of rules in moral judgments, the Lifeline program recognizes the importance of rules in making judgments in general. The Lifeline authors, McPhail, Ungoes-Thomas, and Chapman, state that:

> Proving the Rule? recognizes that one important aspect of becoming a healthy adult is learning to find solutions to the problems that arise for people living in a highly complex and structured society, a society that has many rules and that expects people to assume a variety of often conflicting positions. Being a parent, a worker, a husband or wife, and a driver can present a person with difficult conflict situations. What do you do for example, if your job requires you to go away for a week and your wife or husband needs you at home? Or what do you do when you simply don't feel like doing something that is expected of you in your job; you may be a magistrate or a worker at a germ warfare plant.[48]

Though the Lifeline program seems to be speaking of societal rules, this interpretation would not be wholly fair. Rather, Piaget, Kohlberg, and the Lifeline authors are asserting the following: The morally mature person is the one who autonomously makes principled moral decisions, acts on his own decisions, and is

179

N O T E S

1. For an argument against indoctrination, see John Wilson, "Education and Indoctrination,"Aims in Education, T. H. B. Hollins, ed. (Manchester: University Press, 1964), pp. 24-46.
     Also, John Wilson, "Teaching and Neutrality," Progress and Problems in Moral Education, Monica J. Taylor, ed. (Slough, Berks: NFER Publishing Co., 1975), pp. 113-122.

2. W. R. Niblett, "Some Problems in Moral Education Today," Moral Education in a Changing Society, W. R. Niblett, ed. (London: Faber and Faber, 1963), p. 14.

3. Jean Piaget, The Moral Judgment of the Child, Marjorie Gabain, trans. (New York: The Free Press, 1965), p. 122.

4. Ibid., p. 123.

5. Ibid., p. 162.

6. Ibid., p. 13.

7. Emile Durkheim, Moral Education, E. K. Wilson and H. Schnurer, trans. (New York: Free Press, 1961), p.23.

8. Ibid., p. 24 (my italics).

9. Ibid., p. 26 (my italics).

10. Piaget, The Moral Judgment, p. 9.

11. Inhelder and Piaget, Growth of Logical Thinking, pp. 336-337.

12. J. H. Flavell, The Developmental Psychology of Jean Piaget (Princeton, N. J.: Van Nostrand, 1963), p. 290-291.

13. Piaget, op.cit., p. 102.

14. Ibid., p. 261.

15. Ibid.

16. Ibid., p. 125.

17. Ibid.

18. Ibid., p. 315

19. Ibid.

20. Ibid., p. 316.

21. Ibid., p. 370 (my italics).

22. Ibid., p. 404.

23. This analysis of Kohlberg's theory is derived from the following sources:

Lawrence Kohlberg, "From Is To Ought: How to Commit the Naturalistic Fallacy and Get Away with It in the Study of Moral Development," Cognitive Development and Epistemology, T. Mischel, ed. (New York: Academic Press, 1971), p. 165.
Lawrence Kohlberg, "Moral Stages and Moralization: The Cognitive Developmental Approach." Moral Development and Behavior, Theory, Research, and Social Issues, T. Lickona, ed. (New York: Holt, Rinehart and Winston, 1976), pp. 31-53. Lawrence Kohlberg and Rochelle Mayer, "Development as the Aim of Education," Harvard Educational Review, vol. 42 (1972), pp. 449-496.

24. For some of the Kohlberg moral dilemmas, Nancy Porter and Nancy Taylor, How to Assess the Moral Reasoning of Students (Toronto: The Ontario Institute for Studies in Education, 1972).

25. Kohlberg, "From Is To Ought . . .," p. 169.

26. Ibid., p. 164.

27. A similar result was forthcoming from the Havighurst and Neugarten study of American Indian children using Piagetean moral dilemmas. However, the original Havighurst and Neugarten study used Piaget's dilemmas to determine animism and heteronomy versus autonomy and were considered the most unsuccessful sections of the overall study. Both the original study and a more recent re-evaluation of the original findings by Kohlberg, Havighurst and Neugarten (unpublished) indicate that though development proceeds through early adolescence, thereafter, as expected by Piaget, regression occurs to bring the child into conformity with the

accepted morality, values, and religion of the culture.
Robert J. Havighurst and Bernice L. Neugarten, *American
Indian and White Children* (Chicago, 1955).

28. Lawrence Kohlberg, Peter Scharf, and Joseph Hickey,
"The Justice Structure of the Prison - A Theory and an
Intervention," *The Prison Journal*, vol. LI, no. 2 (1972),
pp. 3-14.

29. Charles Dickens, *Dombey and Son* (New York: New
American Library, 1964), p. 16.

30. Kohlberg, "From Is To Ought . . .", p. 170.

31. *Ibid.*

32. *Ibid.*

33. *Ibid.*

34. *Ibid.*, p. 164.

35. Porter and Taylor, *op.cit.*, p. 17.

36. Kohlberg, "From Is To Ought . . .", p. 165.

37. Porter and Taylor, *op.cit.*, p. 20.

38. Kohlberg, *op.cit.*, p. 200.

39. *Ibid.*, p. 202.

40. *Ibid.*, p. 165.

41. *Ibid.*, p. 206.

42. *Ibid.*, p. 208.

43. Lawrence Kohlberg, "Indoctrination Versus Relativity in Value Education," *Zygon*, vol. 6 (Dec., 1971).

44. Leon Festinger, *A Theory of Cognitive Dissonance*
(Stanford: Stanford University Press, 1957), pp.12-13.

45. Peter McPhail, J. R. Ungoed-Thomas, Hilary Chapman,
Moral Education in the Secondary School (London: Longman, 1972) pp. 23-49.

46. William J. Bennet and Edwin J. Delattre, "A Moral
Education," *American Educator*, vol. 3 (1979), p. 9.

47. For this see Alexander Frazier, Values, Curriculum, and the Elementary School (Boston: Houghton Mifflin Co., 1980), pp. 124-129. Richard H. Hersh, Diana Pritchard Paolitto, Joseph Reimer, Promoting Moral Growth, From Piaget to Kohlberg, New York: Longman, 1979), pp. 209-219.

48. Peter McPhail, J. R. Ungoes-Thomas, Hilary Chapman, Learning to Care: Rationale and Method of the Lifeline Program (Niles, Ill: Argus, 1976), p. 127.

BIBLIOGRAPHY

Books

Bellanca, James A. Values and the Search for Self.
Washington, D. C.: National Education Association, 1975.

Berkowitz, Leonard, The Development of Motives and
Values in the Child, New York: Basic Books, 1964.

Bull, Norman J. Moral Education. London: Routledge
and Kegan Paul, 1969.
     Norman Bull studies the educational implication of
his earlier study of the moral judgments of 7 to 17 year
olds. Included are such topics as external-internal
morality, factors which influence moral development,
e.g., intelligence and religion. Though this is an
early study using Piaget's theory, it still is valuable
for anyone doing an in-depth study of moral development
and education.

Bull, Norman J. Moral Judgment from Childhood to Adolescence. London: Routledge and Kegan Paul, 1969.
     This book presents the results of Bull's 3 year
research project with 360 children and adolescents.
The tests and pictures presented together with the
results at different ages are included. In particular,
Bull studied his subjects' views regarding the value
of life, cheating, stealing, lying, helpfulness, etc.
Furthermore, the person's judgment was correlated with
intelligence, socio-economic class, church attendance,
religious group, and attitudes. The results of this
study are compared with previous empirical studies and
theories.

Chazan, Barry I. and Soltis, Jonas F., eds. Moral
Education. New York: Teachers College Press. 1973.
     The following sections include a wide range of
theoretical essays: "Morality and Philosophy," "Justification in Ethics,""Moral Principles," "Moral Sense
and Autonomy," and "Teaching and Morality."

Damon, William, ed. Moral Development. San Francisco:
Jossey-Bass, Inc., 1978.
     These theoretical essays study how morality devel-
ops through interaction between the child and culture.
In addition to examining the changes in Lawrence Kohlberg's theory, other newer theoretical ways of viewing

185

child-culture interaction are examined, e.g., a socio-analytic theory of moral development and how children's speech reveals their use of moral rules.

DePalma, David J. and Foley, J. M., Moral Development: Current Theory and Research. Hillsdale, N. Y.: Halstead, 1975.

Durkheim, Emile, Moral Education, A Study in the Theory and Application of the Sociology of Education, trans. E. K. Wilson and H. Schnurer, New York: Free Press, 1961 (1925).
    This book has had an exceptionally important role in the history of moral developmental theories. Jean Piaget argues that at the lower stage of moral development, the child's use of rules parallels Durkheim's theory. Though Kohlberg initially rejected the implications of Durkheim's theory, Kohlberg more recently (1978) argues that the indoctrination of certain basic societal rules is necessary. Thus, Kohlberg now seems to accept some of Durkheim's ideas.
    After developing the elements of morality primarily from a sociological perspective, Durkheim devotes the second section to an examination of how these elements develop in the child and how the school can assist such development.

Duska, Ronald and Whelan, Mariellen, Moral Development: A Guide to Piaget and Kohlberg. Ramsey, N. J.: Paulist Press, 1975.
    This popular Guide relates the theories of Piaget and Kohlberg to Christian moral theory and educational practice.

Fraenkel, Jack R. How to Teach about Values: An Analytic Approach. Englewood Cliffs, N. J.: Prentice-Hall, Inc., 1977.

Frazier, Alexander, Values, Curriculum, and the Elementary School. Boston: Houghton Mifflin, 1980.

Graham, Douglas. Moral Learning and Development: Theory and Research. London: B. T. Batsford, Ltd., 1972.
    This comprehensive account of psychological theories of moral learning and development includes the contributions of Freud, Skinner, Bandura and Walters, Piaget, Kohlberg, etc. It examines how intelligence, sex, religion, social class, parental training, etc.

affect moral learning and development. Graham includes a number of interesting sections which often are omitted from general overviews, e.g., types of moral character and "people without conscience."

Hall, Robert T. and Davis, John J. Moral Education in Theory and Practice. Buffalo, N. Y.: Prometheus Books, 1975.
    The first sections of this well written book analyze philosophical and psychological concepts, principles, and theories of the moral domain and moral education. The last sections connect theory with practice and examine four methods of moral education--the case study method, analysis, games, and simulation.

Hart, Gordon M. Value Clarification for Counselors: How Counselors, Social Workers, Psychologists, and Other Human Service Workers Can Use Available Techniques. Springfield, Ill: Charles C. Thomas Publ., 1978.

Hawley, Robert C. Value Exploration Through Role Playing: Practical Strategies for Use in the Classroom. New York: Hart Publishing Co., Inc., 1975.
    Hawley's guides to role-playing techniques is particularly suitable for junior and senior high school students. While presenting some tips on "how to do it," Hawley includes numerous examples of role playing strategies for value development.

Hawley, Robert C. and Isabel L. Human Values in the Classroom. New York: Hart Publishing Co., Inc., 1975.

Hennessy, Thomas C., ed. Values and Moral Development. Ramsey, N. J.: Paulist Press, 1979.
    These analytical essays and responses mainly stress Piaget's and Kohlberg's theories. In addition to studying value and moral education in terms of curriculum, counselling, and cognitive development, there is an essay on structural stages of religious faith.

Hersh, Richard H., Pritchard Paolitto, Diana, and Reimer, Joseph. Promoting Moral Growth, from Piaget to Kohlberg. New York: Longman Inc., 1979.
    A clear introduction to the theoretical and practical aspects of Piaget's and Kohlberg's moral development theories.

Hersh, Richard H., Miller, John P., and Fielding, Glen D. Models of Moral Education, and Appraisal. New York: Longman Inc., 1980.

This is a clear, concise, and brief presentation of six moral education models. It includes practical applications and criticism of each model.

Hirst, Paul H. _Moral Education in a Secular Society_. London: University of London Press, Ltd., 1974.
   After analyzing the relationship between contemporary secular morality and the religious moral tradition, Hirst, an English philosopher, suggests approaches to moral education in secular schools.

Kay, William. _Moral Development_. London: George Allen and Unwin Ltd., rev. 1970.
   After presenting major empirical and theoretical studies of moral development, Kay argues that a comprehensive plan of moral development based on an attitudinal model can assist teachers in their search for techniques to motivate students' moral development.

Ladenburg, Thomas and Muriel, and Scharf, Peter. _Moral Education: A Classroom Workbook_. Davis, CA: Responsible Action, 1978.
   Though the authors claim this workbook is based on Kohlberg's theory, many of the examples and exercises do not necessarily require acceptance of Kohlberg. The practical applications and strategies are excellent.

Lerner, Max. _Values in Education: Notes Toward a Values Philosophy_. Bloomington, Ind.: Phi Delta Kappan, 1976.
   A general assessment of the development of values and education for social change.

Lickona, Thomas, ed. _Moral Development and Behavior: Theory, Research, and Social Issues_. New York: Holt, Rinehart, and Winston, 1976.
   Each of this book's scholarly, comprehensive essays studies a major theory of aspect of moral development and moral education. For example, in addition to Lawrence Kohlberg's cognitive-developmental approach, such theoretical topics as social-learning theory; cross-cultural perspectives; empathy; psychoanalysis and moral development, etc. are systematically studied. Another section includes an essay evaluating research on moral judgments and development. The Burton article takes another look at the Hartshorne and May study of honesty and dishonesty and correlates it with more recent empirical research. The last section of the book "Morality and Social Issues," includes essays on a number of topics which have remained of perennial interest both to the general public and scholar. For example,

one article presents a model for understanding how television is a moral educator. Huston and Dorte study why bystanders are responsive. Finally, this excellent volume includes a lengthy bibliography.

Lockwood, Alan L. Values Education and the Study of Other Cultures. Washington, D. C.: National Education Association, 1976.

Macaulay, J. and Berkowitz, Altruism and Helping Behavior: Social Psychological Studies of Some Antecedents and Consequences. New York: Academic Press, 1970.
    A scholarly, in-depth study of various aspects of altruism and helping behavior.

McPhail, Peter, Ungoed-Thomas, J. R., and Chapman, Hilary. Learning to Care: Rationale and Method of the Lifeline Program. Niles, Ill: Argus Communications, 1975.
    The authors first summarize the results of their extensive research project which identified adolescents' needs. In the second part they present a program of moral education based on adolescent needs and the authors' aim, "providing education for choice." Included in their practical techniques and sample lessons are the teacher's role; recognizing other people's viewpoint; sensitivity; the consequences of acting; proving moral rules; etc.
    Other titles are included in this series. Each general title includes a number of pamphlets which expand the theme. The following are some of the titles and pamphlets:
    In Other People's Shoes: Sensitivity
    Proving the Rule?
        1. Rules and Individuals.
        2. What Do You Expect?
        3. Who Do You Think I am?
        4. In Whose Interests?
        5. Why Should I?
    What Would You Have Done?
        Birth Day, South Africa, 1904.
        Solitary Confinement, England, 1917.
        Arrest! Amsterdam, 1944.
        Street Scene, Los Angeles, 1965.
        Tragedy, Vietnam, 1966.
        Gale in the Hospital, 1969.

Moral Education in the Secondary School. London: Longman, 1972.

After describing their research of adolescents'
views of morality and helping behavior, the authors
present materials and techniques developed from the
research outlined.

Mosher, Ralph L. , Moral Education, a First Generation
of Research and Development. New York: Praeger Publishers, 1980.
    The readings in this book include theoretical,
empirical, curriculum, and other practical studies of
Lawrence Kohlberg's theory of moral cognitive development.

Mussen, Paul and Eisenberg-Berg, Nancy, Roots of Caring,
Sharing, and Helping. San Francisco: W. M. Freeman and
Co. , 1977.
    In their exploration of how cultural values affect
a child's helping behavior and how child-rearing practices foster prosocial behavior, the authors study the
development of altruism, generosity, personal consideration, and sharing. Using many examples from other cultures and literature, various current theories and empirical research suggest how prosocial behavior is
learned and can be modified by parents, educators, and
the media.

Paterson, R. W. K. Values, Education and the Adult.
London: Routledge and Kegan Paul, 1979.

Perry, Jr., William G., Forms of Intellectual and Ethical Development in the College Years. New York: Holt,
Rinehart, and Winston, Inc., 1968.
    After tracing a sample of Harvard University stud-
ents through their four years of intellectual and value
development, Perry postulates nine positions of development. In the last chapter, Perry presents the study's
implications for college teaching.

Piaget, Jean   The Moral Judgment of the Child. Marjorie Gabain, trans. New York: Free Press, 1965.
    This classical seminal work provides the basis for
a substantial part of present theories and empirical research on the development of moral judgments. The
first section of the book investigates the rules of
children's games, children's use of game rules, peer
pressure on children to accept game rules, and the
transmission of rules from one generation of children
to the next. Using stories and open-ended questions,
Piaget analyzes how children's judgments of lying,

cheating, punishment, authority, and responsibility develop with age. Finally, Piaget compares his developmental theory with social psychological theories e.g.,
especially that of Durkheim, and philosophical concepts
and principles, especially those of Kant. This book is
must reading for anyone studying the moral development
of children.

Raths, Louis E., Harmin, Merrill, and Simon, Sidney B.
Values and Teaching: Working with Values in the Classroom. Columbus, Ohio: Charles E. Merrill Publ. Co.,
1966.
    This was the first book on values clarification in
which the authors introduce their theory of values and
the methodology of values clarification.

Rosen, High. The Development of Sociomoral Knowledge,
a Cognitive-Structural Approach. New York: Columbia University Press 1980.
    After examining Piaget's and Kohlberg's theories
of the development of moral judgments, Rosen examines
1) the various criticism of Kohlberg's theory and 2) how
this approach to sociomoral development can be used in
the helping professions.

Scharf, Peter. Moral Education. Davis, CA: Responsible Action, 1978.
    This introduction is based on Kohlberg's theory.

Silver, Michael, Values Education. Washington, D. C.:
National Education Association, 1976.

Simon, Sidney B., Hawley, Robert C., and Britton, David
D. Composition for Personal Growth: Values Clarification Through Writing. New York: Hart Publishing Co.,
1973.
    As the title notes, this values clarification
strategy guide is devoted to the teaching of values
through English composition.

Simon, Sidney B. and Olds Saly Wedkos, Helping Your
Child Learn Right From Wrong: A Guide to Values Clarification. New York: McGraw-Hill Book Co., 1977.

Sizer, Nancy F. and Theodore R. Moral Education, Five
Lectures. Cambridge, Mass.: Harvard University Press,
1970.
    These readable general essays were written by lead-
ing figures, e.g., Kohlberg, Bettelheim.

191

Stephenson, Geoffrey M., _The Development of Conscience_.
London: Routledge and Kegan Paul, 1966.

Stiles, Lindley J. and Johnson, Bruce D., eds. _Morality Examined: Guidelines for Teachers_. Princeton, N. J.:
Princeton Book Co., Publ., 1977.

Sugarman, Barry. _The School and Moral Development_.
London: Croom Helm Ltd., 1975.
     Looking at the school institution from a socio-
logical perspective, Barry examines how the school acts
as a socializing and moral development agent.

Taylor, Monica J., ed. _Progress and Problems in Moral Education_. Slough, Berks: NFER Publishing, Ltd., 1975.

Wilson, John. _Practical Methods of Moral Education_.
London: Heinemann Educational Books, 1972.
     Wilson argues that though considerable practical
material on moral education is available, teachers have
difficulty deciding what they should be doing. Thus,
Wilson provides a rationale and logic of moral education
methods, and criteria for selecting methods and materials.

Wilson, John. _Reason and Morals_. Cambridge: University
Press, 1961.
     This introduction to analytical moral philosophy
aims to assist the layman in resolving moral dilemmas.
In addition, this early book is an excellent preface to
Wilson's other books on moral education.

Wilson, John, Williams, Norman, and Sugarman, Barry.
Introduction to Moral Education. Hammandsworth, Middle-
sex, Eng: Penguin Books, Ltd., 1967.
     This highly respected book provides an interdis-
ciplinary approach to the foundations of moral education. It studies philosophic concepts, e.g., prudence,
being reasonable; what is meant by moral education; the
relationship between indoctrination and freedom; assessment of the 'morally educated' person; psychologists'
contribution to moral education, e.g., conscience, the
psychopath; what the sociologist has to contribute; and
finally practical implications.

Windmiller, Myra, Lambert, Natine, and Turiel, Elliot,
eds. _Moral Development and Socialization_. Boston:
Allyn and Bacon, Inc., 1980.
     Though many of these essays include a section on
applications, they primarily deal with theoretical

aspects of value and moral development. In addition
to a number of Kohlbergian essays, e.g., on the relationship between moral judgment and behavior, there are
essays on social learning theory and psychoanalytical
contributions to moral education.

Articles by and about Kohlberg's theory of moral development.

Alston, William P., "Comments on Kohlberg's 'From Is to
Ought'", Cognitive Development and Epistemology, Theodore
Mischel, ed. New York: Academic Press, 1971. pp.269-
284.

Blatt, Moshe and Kohlberg, Lawrence, "The Effects of
Classroom Moral Discussion upon Children's Level of
Moral Judgments," Journal of Moral Education, vol. 4
(1975), pp. 129-162.

Bressler, Marvin, "Kohlberg and the Resolution of Moral
Conflict," New York University Quarterly, vol. VII (1976)
pp. 2-8.

Conroy, Anne R. and Burton, John K., "The Trouble with
Kohlberg: A Critique," The Educational Forum, vol. XLV
(1980), pp. 43-55.

Diorio, Joseph A., "Cognitive Universalism and Cultural
Relativity in Moral Education," Educational Philosophy
and Theory, vol. 8 (1976), pp. 33-53.

Edwards, Carolyn P., "Societal Complexity and Moral Development: A Kenyan Study," Ethos, vol. 3 (Winter 1975),
pp. 505-527.

Fishkin, J., Kenison, K., and MacKinnon, C., "Moral
Reasoning and Political Ideology," Journal of Personality and Social Psychology, vol. 27 (1973), pp. 109-119.

Gibbs, John C., "Kohlberg's Stages of Moral Judgment: A
Constructive Change," Harvard Educational Review, vol.
47 (1977), pp. 43-61.

Haan, Norma, Langer, Jonas, and Kohlberg, Lawrence,
"Family Patterns of Moral Reasoning," Child Development,
vol. 47 (1976), pp. 1204-1206.

Haan, N., Smith, M. B., and Block, J., "The Moral Reasoning of Young Adults, Political-Social Behavior, and Family Background, and Personality Correlates," Journal of Personality and Social Psychology, vol. 10 (1968), pp. 183-201.

Kohlberg, Lawrence. "Early Education: A Cognitive-Developmental View," Child Development, vol. 39 (1968), pp. 1013-1062.

"Education, Moral Development, and Faith," Journal of Moral Education, vol. 4 (1974), pp. 5-16.

"From Is to Ought: How to Commit the Naturalistic Fallacy and Get Away with It in the Study of Moral Development," Cognitive Development and Epistemology, Theodore Mischel, ed. New York: Academic Press, 1971. pp. 151-235.

"Indoctrination Versus Relativity in Value Education," Zygon: Journal of Religion and Science, vol. 6 (1971), pp. 285-310.

"Moral Education: A Response to Thomas Sobol," Educational Leadership, vol. 38 (1980), pp. 19-23.

"The Moral Atmosphere of the School," The Unstudied Curriculum: Its Impact on Children, N. V. Overly, ed. Washington, D. C.: Assoc. for Supervision and Curriculum Development, 1970, pp. 104-127.

"Stages and Aging in Moral Development - Some Speculations," Gerontology, vol. 13 (1973), pp. 497-502.

"The Child as Moral Philosopher," Psychology Today, vol. 2 (September 1968), pp. 25-30.

"The Development of Children's Orientation Toward a Moral Order, I. Sequence in the Development of Moral Thought," Vita Humana, vol. 6 (1963), pp. 11-33.

Kohlberg, Lawrence and Gilligan, Carol, "The Adolescent as a Philosopher: The Discovery of the Self in a Post-Conventional World," Daedalus, vol. 100 (1971), pp. 1051-1086.

Kohlberg, Lawrence and Kramer, R., "Continuities and Discontinuities in Childhood and Adult Moral Development," Human Development, vol. 12 (1969), pp. 93-120.

Kohlberg, Lawrence, and Mayer, Rochelle, "Development as
the Aim of Education," Harvard Educational Review, vol.
42 (1972), pp. 449-496.

Kohlberg, Lawrence, Scharf, Peter, and Hickey, Joseph,
"The Justice Structure of the Prison - A Theory and an
Intervention," The Prison Journal, vol. LI (1972), pp.
3-14.

Kohlberg, Lawrence and Turiel, Elliot, "Moral Develop-
ment and Moral Education," Psychology and Educational
Practice, Gerald S. Lesser, ed. Glenview, Ill.: Scott
Foresman & Co., 1971, pp. 410-465.

Kohlberg, Lawrence, with Phillip Whitten, "Understanding the Hidden Curriculum," Learning (1972), pp.10-14.

Kurtines, William and Greif, Esther Blan, "The Development of Moral Thought: Review and Evaluation of Kohlberg's Approach," Psychological Bulletin, vol. 81,
(1974), pp. 453-470.

McGeorge, C., "Situational Variation in Level of Moral
Judgment," The British Journal of Educational Psychology,
vol. 44 (1974), pp. 116-122.

Oldham, Sally, "Critique of the Original Moral Judgment
Instrument Developed by Lawrence Kohlberg," Journal of
Social Studies Research, vol. 1 (1977), pp. 1-9.

Peters, R. S., "Moral Development: A Plea for Pluralism," Cognitive Development and Epistemology, Theodore
Mischel, ed. New York: Academic Press, (1971), pp.237-
267.

"The Place of Kohlberg's Theory in Moral Education,"
Journal of Moral Education, vol. 7 (1978), pp.147-157.

Reimer, Joseph, "Moral Education: The Just Community
Approach," Phi Delta Kappan, vol. 62 (1981), pp.485-487.

Rest, James, "Developmental Psychology as a Guide to
Value Education: A Review of 'Kohlbergian' Programs,"
Review of Educational Research, vol. 44 (1974), pp.241-
259.

Rest, James, Turiel, Elliot, and Kohlberg, Lawrence,
"Levels of Moral Development as a Determinant of Preference and Comprehension of Moral Judgments," Journal

of Personality, vol. 37 (1969) pp. 225-252.

Sichel, Betty A., "A Critical Study of Kohlberg's Theory of the Development of Moral Judgments," Proceedings of the Philosophy of Education Society (1976), pp.209-220.

"Can Kohlberg Respond to Critics?" Educational Theory, vol. 26 (1976), pp. 337-347.

"The Relation Between Moral Judgment and Moral Behavior in Kohlberg's Theory of the Development of Moral Judgments," Educational Philosophy and Theory, vol. 8 (1976), pp. 55-67.

Hamm, Cornel M., "The Content of Moral Education, or In Defense of the 'Bag of Virtues'", School Review, vol. 85 (1977), pp. 218-228.

Simpson, E. L., "Moral Development Research" A Case Study of Scientific Cultural Bias," Human Development, vol. 17 (1974), pp. 81-106.

Trainer, F. E., "A Critical Analysis of Kohlberg's Contributions to the Study of Moral Thought," Journal for the Theory of Social Behavior, vol. 7 (1977), pp.41-63.

Turiel, Elliot, "An Experimental Test of the Sequentiality of Developmental Stages in the Child's Moral Judgments," Journal of Personality and Social Psychology, vol. 3 (1966), pp. 611-618.

Articles on Moral Learning, Development, and Education.

Bennett, William J. and Delattre, Edwin J. "A Moral Education," American Education, vol. 3 (1979), pp.6-9.

"Moral Education in the Schools," The Public Interest, vol. 50 (1978), pp. 81-98.

Brandt, Ronald S., "On Moral/Civic Education" Educational Leadership. (1977), pp. 487-494.

Etzioni, Amitai, "Can Schools Teach Kids Values?" Today's Education, vol. 66 (1977), pp. 29-38.

"Do as I Say, not as I do." New York Times Magazine (September 26, 1976), pp. 44-45+.

Gash, High, "Moral Judgment: A Comparison of Two

Theoretical Approaches," <u>Genetic Psychology Monographs</u>, vol. 93 (1976), pp. 91-111.

Lockwood, Alan L., "A Critical View of Values Clarification," <u>Teachers College Record</u>, vol. 77 (1975), pp.35-50.

"The Effects of Values Clarification and Moral Development Curricula on School-Age Subjects: A Critical Review of Recent Research," <u>Review of Educational Research</u> vol. 48 (1978), pp. 325-364.

Mosher, Ralph, "Moral Education: Seven Years Before the Mast," <u>Educational Leadership</u>, vol. 38 (1980), pp.12-15.

Ravitch, Diane, "Moral Education and the Schools," <u>Commentary</u>, vol. 56 (1973), pp. 62-66.

Sobol, Thomas, "An Administrator Looks at Moral Education: And if I ask these things, will ye still call me friend?" <u>Educational Leadership</u>, vol. 38 (1980), pp. 16-17.

Stahl, Robert, "Working with Values and Moral Issues in Content-Centered Science Classrooms," <u>Science Education</u>, vol. 63 (1979), pp. 183-194.

Thomas, Donald and Richards, Margaret, "Ethics Education is Possible!" <u>Phi Delta Kappan</u>, vol. 60 (1979), pp. 579-582.

Williams, David M. and Wright, Ian, "Values and Moral Education: Analyzing Curriculum Materials," <u>The Social Studies</u>, vol. 33 (1969), pp. 41-47.

Wynne, Edward A., "The Declining Character of American Youth," <u>American Educator</u>, vol. 3 (1979), pp. 29-32.

<u>Periodicals and Issues Devoted to Moral Development and Education</u>.

<u>Journal of Moral Education</u>.

<u>Moral Education Forum</u>.

<u>Phi Delta Kappan</u>, vol. LVI, no. 10 (June 1975).

<u>Social Education</u>, vol. 40, no. 4 (April 1976), general topic, "Cognitive-Developmental Approach to Moral Education."

Teachers College Record, vol. 80, no. 3 (February 1979), devoted to education and values.

The Monist, vol. 58, no. 4 (October 1974), general topic, "The Philosophy of Moral Education."

Theory Into Practice, vol. XIV, no. 4 (October 1975), general topic, "Moral Education."

Theory Into Practice, vol. XVI, no. 2 (April 1977), general topic, "Moral Development."